Reputation 360

Creating power through personal branding

What people are saying...

"Personal brand matters. Lida's approach is fresh, effective, engaging and nets tangible results."

Randy Wilhelm
CEO, NetTrekker

"Lida challenged us to seriously consider our personal brands and how we differentiate ourselves amongst the crowd of providers. Lida's credibility is enhanced by her authenticity and vast experience. Most importantly, she walks her talk and lives it out with passion!"

Mark Gouin
Senior Vice President, Wells Fargo

"Lida has given us a powerful tool through her personal branding training. She has given me the power to find the right people and places where I can flourish in a fulfilling career."

Jeff Knott
Associate, Wall Street Warfighters Foundation

"Over the last couple of years, Lida has developed the personal branding work for me and industry leaders I know. She is also the person I trusted to help position the founder of one of our companies as a leading expert in her industry. She has been highly effective for me and the people I refer to her."

Kevin Custer
Founding Principal, ARC Capital Development

"Tackling the branding exercises with Lida was a complete eye-opener. She helped me to see strengths I didn't know I had, and to find new and better ways to articulate key messages about my firm. Working with Lida was a game-changing experience that has helped me to grow my business."

Charlene Blohm, President
C. Blohm & Associates, Inc.

"Lida walked us through every step of our rebranding effort and offered unique insights and solutions. I would hire Lida again, and refer any business to her that seeks the clarity and results of a true experienced professional!"

Stephanie Klein
CEO, The Experience Factor

"Lida Citroen's dedication to the success of disabled US veterans is immeasurable. She provides the necessary tools for a successful Wall Street career to graduates of our program. It's essential training as they begin the conversion to private sector careers."

John P. Jones
Executive Director, Wall Street Warfighters Foundation

"Everyone deserves to craft and maintain a brand that reflects their core values, skills and goals, and Lida knows exactly how to help anyone make immediate changes to create a lasting impact on their personal brand."

Jennifer Petit
Staff Project Manager, Qwest

"Lida's professionalism and talent as a brand strategist is inspiring. I value her input and ideas, and she has the amazing gift of helping one take their vision and put wheels on it. She has challenged me to think bigger and bolder about where I want to take my most important project of the year!"

Lethia Owens
CEO, Lethia Owens International

"I feel I am a better leader and follower after spending time under Lida's spell."

Chad Thorpe
Senior Vice President, StarTek

"What a professional! Lida brings a wealth of tools and expertise and her own gentle but consistent coaching. I highly recommend LIDA360!"

Caroline Turner
Principal, DifferenceWORKS, LLC

"Lida knows her stuff and walks her talk. Her own personal brand is clear, consistent, professional, and remarkable. If you need to know about personal branding, I highly recommend Lida!"

Dr. Bret Simmons
Associate Professor of Management
University of Nevada at Reno

"My experience with Lida's personal branding program was truly life-changing! I now can be intentional about the message I deliver to the public and am attracting new clients to my business who appreciate the strengths I offer."

Beth O'Neill
Principal, Planning Solutions

"Lida presented her Personal Branding program to my undergraduate class of seniors at Colorado State University. Most (of my students) said they'd never thought of personal branding, how they appear on their social media pages, and were definitely interested in understanding more about how to present themselves and build an authentic self-presentation. She's super, and what she's presenting is very relevant, timely, and clear."

Zinta Byrne, Ph.D.
Associate Professor
Colorado State University

"If you truly want better results, call Lida. She has a great gift for identifying opportunities and then lays out direct, concise paths to get there. Her vast experience serves her well. She has a dynamic combination of intelligence, listening skills and passion that allows her to read situations quickly and accurately. If you want a different outcome, Lida can help you get there."

Carrie Mesch
President, MESCH Commercial Real Estate

"Lida helped me bring focus to my brand that's clear and easy for people to understand. I also think more about how people feel versus what they think when I walk away from a meeting with them. It's made such a big difference in the positive responses I get from clients and colleagues."

Margie Adams
Owner, EMERGE

"The most admirable aspect of Lida's personal branding process is that she not only talks the talk but she walks the walk. I highly recommend Lida for anyone who needs to ensure they convey the right message and anyone making a career transition."

Jon Arnold
Associate, Wall Street Warfighters Foundation

"Lida is a dynamic and powerful communicator who possesses the gift of being able to make complex subjects understandable. She has taught and encouraged me to meet challenges that I had never before thought possible."

Lori Frisher
Account Executive, Integra Telecom

"Lida brings clarity, focus and sense of direction with powerful insight. She is able to translate thoughts, feelings and behaviors into concise messaging that truly reflects your brand."

Carol Alm
President, Carol Ratcliffe Alm & Associates

"Lida knows branding. In a very well organized (and painless) process, she pinpoints your personal brand DNA and makes actionable recommendations for strengthening and moving your brand in the direction you want to move. I thoroughly enjoyed working with Lida. I trust her expertise and admire her approach with clients."

Kirsty Wertz
Vice President of Marketing, NetTrekker

"Lida has been invaluable in helping me with my personal branding and getting my name 'out there' for my business. Lida is a true professional with a thorough knowledge of personal branding and its importance in today's business world."

Billy Van Heusen, Sr.
former Denver Broncos player, NFL Alumni

Reputation 360

Creating power through personal branding

Lida Citroën
Principal, LIDA360, LLC
Corporate and Personal Branding Expert

ℙℙ
Palisades Publishing

Reputation 360: Creating power through personal branding

Published by Palisades Publishing, Greenwood Village, CO

First Edition

ISBN 978-0-9831690-0-0

Library of Congress Control Number: 2011924228

Cover design and graphics by Scott Maiwald.
Editing by Patti M. Thorn.

Printed in the U.S.A.

Dedicated to Scott, Clark and Beau—the most important people in my life. Thank you for giving me the love, support and encouragement to be who I need to be!

TABLE OF CONTENTS

"Promise me you'll always remember: You're braver than you believe, and stronger than you seem, and smarter than you think."

- Christopher Robin to Pooh

Introduction

Just like you, I have had wonderful opportunities in my life—and many challenges. I've done amazing things that won awards—and I've burned bridges due to careless behavior. I've had a career of creating, becoming, losing and learning, and today I am a reflection of it all.

What I also have, like you, is a reputation. I created some of that reputation through my actions, with little thought. Other aspects I designed intentionally to ensure that the people who matter to me find me valuable and relevant. That's the part I'm here to share with you and teach you how to create.

By picking up this book, you have taken the first bold step: You are officially on the personal branding journey. There will be no turning back, no second-guessing over every choice you make. You will no longer strive for validation from others; you will find confirmation of your decisions within yourself. My hope is that through this book you will find your authentic voice and passion and learn how to effectively and efficiently communicate them to others so they will create powerful opportunities for you.

In my career as a corporate and personal brand strategist and counsel for executives of Fortune 500 companies, I have had the honor and pleasure of helping all kinds of people: leaders in innovative education technology; venture capitalists with a passion for sustainability and impact investing; outspoken advocates for the advancement and empowerment of American adolescents; cancer survivors; disabled U.S. war veterans; coaches; consultants; moms, dads and their college-age kids. My clients aren't celebrities, but they are well known in their respective industries.

They all realize the importance of managing their reputations and building authentic relationships though personal branding. Throughout this book, I will share some of their stories—their struggles and accomplishments—to illustrate how people come to the realization that they need personal branding help and the results they can achieve from that guidance.

My greatest success has always been in promoting companies, products or people that come from a place of authenticity and genuineness— realness, in other words. A big part of the work I do is to help clients bring forward that authenticity and market it to the right audience.

In this book, I will share my views on personal branding and the processes that will enable you to become the person you are meant to be, to attract the clients and relationships you desire and to draw opportunities to you more easily. Your personal branding journey starts with you and ends with you. In between, we focus on creating an intentional and fulfilling set of action steps that will bring you more joy and wealth and the ability to craft your own legacy.

This book will help you lay the foundation to control, direct and own your reputation. How other people see you directly impacts the value they assign you, and your ability to influence and, in some cases, even manipulate that perception directly affects the opportunities that you're given in your career, your relationships and your life. Owning responsibility for your reputation and managing the way that you're perceived are critical, for any person at any level of business and on any individual journey to promote their value. Learning how to show up with intention and focus, creates the ability to bring your authentic self to every situation you encounter.

My hope is that you will find what you need in this book, and will be inspired and motivated to help others learn how to maximize their personal brand. Together, we can accomplish great things if we all feel valued and empowered.

Enjoy!

Lida Citroën

1

What is personal branding?

Tom Peters introduced us to the concept of the personal brand in an article he wrote in Fast Company Magazine in the mid-1970s. The article pointed to the fact that we spend billions and billions of dollars branding corporations, products and services, and yet we don't teach the power of individuals to own their reputations and to create an expectation of experience with their target audience.

Since then, the term personal branding has come to mean many things. Some people call personal branding the technique you use to package yourself. Others say it's what public relations professionals do for celebrities to make them marketable as spokespeople. Still others refer to interviewing skills, image consulting and even portrait photography as personal branding.

Most of these descriptions miss the mark. Personal branding is not just about designing "packaging" for yourself or selling yourself as something you are not. Your personal brand is your reputation. It identifies what makes you unique and clearly communicates that uniqueness to an audience that needs you.

A brand is not something you can just put on paper, like a logo or a glossy photo; it has to be expressed in your actions. A brand needs to represent a set of values, promises and expectations and meet those expectations at nearly every step. Branding gives experience to something intangible;

it gives names to the qualities I feel when I work or interact with you. Branding is all about feelings and emotions. Unlike marketing, which is when we direct an audience to action (buy now, act fast, use this coupon, call today…), branding sets the emotional expectations and promises between you and your target audience.

Everyone has a personal brand, because we're all known for something. You may not be known for what you want to be known for, but you are known for something. Your reputation may have been the guiding force behind most of your success to date, or it may have been what has been holding you back from achieving your dreams.

Ultimately, your brand is your legacy. It is the way you are known today, and how you will be remembered when you leave. Your legacy is the most real representation of how you lived, behaved and interacted with others, and how they felt about you.

2

Why you need a positive personal brand

As human beings, we instinctively judge people—it's our nature. We are judgmental creatures by DNA. And that judgment is important. For instance, if somebody walks toward you on the street, you must quickly size up whether that person is someone to fear or someone who might need help. Similarly, in a work situation, you need to judge whether your colleagues can keep your confidences and be trusted with sensitive information. Judgment, in this sense, is the instinctual "gut feeling" we have about others, right or wrong.

In forming judgments about those we know we look specifically for what we believe to be "normal" for that person. (This is particularly true in studying body language, which we will discuss a bit later on.) Is that person normally grouchy and arrogant? Is she usually cheerful and upbeat? "Norming" is what enables us to relate to each other in ways that feel safe and predictable. No one can be perfect all the time—we all have bad days. When I see someone I know to be generous, happy and approachable screaming at a checkout clerk in the grocery store, I don't suddenly perceive him to be arrogant, stubborn and loud. Instead, I write his behavior off as him "having a bad day." On the other hand, if I begin to see that behavior repeat itself, I question my belief about that person and begin to see the new behavior as normal, causing me to see him in a completely different light.

The fact that we judge other people is not a bad thing. But you want to make sure that you are being judged for your true value and in a way that reflects who you truly are, rather than leave it up to chance. This is what personal branding is all about: ensuring that others see you in a way that is consistent with your values, beliefs and the perception you want to create.

There are many reasons people look to personal branding. Maybe you're looking for a new job and want to be perceived in a certain way. Maybe you're not feeling fulfilled in your work and believe that if others saw and appreciated your value, your work life would improve. Maybe you would like to find new ways of engaging with customers, or maybe you don't know who your customers are. Perhaps you are simply seeking a new and different way of leaving your mark on the world.

When you take the time to define and build the reputation you desire and create your personal brand around your authentic skills and values, your target audience is more likely to know who you are, what you do best and why they need you. Personal branding will help you no matter where you are in life: just graduating from college and starting your career, beginning an entrepreneurial venture or maintaining a well-established business as an accountant, lawyer, decorator or teacher.

Here are some of the reasons to develop a personal brand:

- **You'll live with more authenticity.** Personal branding is about owning your own space, your own voice, and feeling empowered in the uniqueness you bring to the world. For this reason, we always start with authenticity. Authenticity is what makes you you. It is the genuine you that sometimes hides because you are unsure, unaware or inhibited. You are not like anyone else. Only you possess the combination of values, skills, beliefs and experiences that make you the person you are. When you can recognize your values (and your weaknesses) and project your authentic self to others, they begin to see you for who you truly are and appreciate the value you contribute to the experience. In turn, you find it takes less effort to decide how, where and when to engage with others, because you always come from a place of sincerity and genuineness.

- **You'll be distinguished from the competition.** Setting yourself apart from others who might offer similar value allows you to avoid the "commodity sale," where your audience chooses based on price alone. Here's an example: If you go to the grocery store looking for laundry detergent and you don't care about a specific brand—if the brands don't mean different and compelling things to you, if you consider all laundry detergent to be created equal and expect they will all deliver the same result—how do you choose? Most often, you will buy the least expensive one. Similarly, if you are not seen as unique, different, compelling and relevant to your employer or potential employer, then you leave to chance the possibility that she might choose someone else for a promotion or new job based only on who's the cheapest to hire. That's not how any of us wants to compete! We don't want to be chosen because we're the least expensive solution among a lineup of options. If that's the case, we risk always competing in that manner and never moving ahead.

- **You will become known for something.** When you sell something, you must have a firm grasp on what separates it from the others. What is the unique selling proposition? The same goes for people. If you have a strong personal brand, your audience begins to see you as a visionary, leader or collaborator, and you become more valuable. You become visible for qualities you have intentionally designed and put forth through your actions and are no longer just another faceless commodity among many.

- **You'll create an emotional connection with your target audience.** On paper you might look fantastic, but how I feel about you as a person will lead me to hire, promote or buy from you. On the other end of every purchase is a person, a human being. As humans, we act on emotion. Remember the last time you bought something you didn't need? Often, we purchase something because the emotional side of our brain gets wrapped up in soaking in the experience. Retailers count on this! They create emotional experiences in their stores—from the edgy, clean, creative feel of an Apple store to the sexy, expensive, exclusive ambience of a BMW showroom—and we're drawn in. We engage and spend when we feel that emotional connection.

- **Branding is about emotions.** It sets the expectation for the emotional benefit our audience will gain from working or being with us.

- **You'll become more focused, more intentional and, therefore, more efficient.** A strong and powerful personal brand lives through intentionally promoting its value at every touch point, from how you interact and engage with others in person (including the words you choose and the way you dress) to the way you present yourself online in social media. This means that before you can project a brand, you first must think about who you are: your goals, your desired reputation, your successes and your challenges. Once you determine these, making decisions on a daily basis becomes infinitely easier, faster and more rewarding.

- **Your target audience will become more evident.** When you build a personal brand, the process requires you to look at the audiences who need to find you compelling and relevant. This focuses your efforts from "anyone who could possibly buy from me" to a targeted group of individuals who understand and want what you have to offer. The foundation for personal branding is based on the Laws of Attraction—what you focus on, you will attract. Theories on the laws of attraction (in the realms of physical science, sociology and psychology) date back to the early 20th century. The basic premise is that if you think positively and with intention, you can manifest greater opportunity than if you dwell in the negative or neglect to think with intention. By taking control and ownership of your personal brand—your reputation, destiny and legacy—you can begin to attract the people and opportunities that align with your vision. If you neglect your personal brand, you leave to random "luck" what you might attract, positive or negative. If done well, your return on investment (ROI) increases and your effort decreases.

- **You'll build credibility.** A personal brand allows you to build credibility because the more you're known for something and the more you fulfill that expectation, the more you build integrity around the promises you make. You can't sell "trust." It's like telling someone you are a good kisser: that's for the other person to decide, not you. But if you are valued and trusted—if you've established credibility—people want to be around you and do business with you. Being trusted by clients, peers and colleagues is critical and is achieved by paying attention to your personal branding and delivering on the promise of that brand at all times.

- **You'll make it easy for others to offer you opportunities.** When your personal brand is clearly defined, intentionally marketed and targeted to a specific audience, your audience knows just what you stand for and can easily understand how you might help them. Likewise, your audience learns how they can help you.

A brand is a promise of the future. If you have branded yourself and intentionally and consistently positioned that brand, you will receive recognition for your accomplishments and contributions.

3

Important elements to building your personal brand: The four C's and an A

There are four C's and an A to remember when building a successful personal brand. First, your brand needs to be clear. It's up to you to clearly articulate to others what makes you unique. If you don't clearly communicate your value, you could fall victim to the commodity sale (described in the last chapter) or, worse yet, to a position of irrelevance. Let's say that I'm considering two interior designers to work on my house, and they both have appropriate skills: They both belong to the right associations, and they both have the same number of years of experience. But one of them is known for being fun to work with and offers great suggestions. She makes me feel like she understands me; she knows my personality, and I won't feel bad asking dumb questions. Also, she has flair and a style that I can relate to. All of a sudden, in my mind, she's not measured side by side with that other interior designer. She has value and uniqueness: She's branded, and she's somebody I want to work with. I will even pay a little bit more for the opportunity to work with her.

Studies show that people are willing to pay nine percent to twelve percent more for a brand that they perceive as different from the others, a brand they know and trust. It's why many women walk into the laundry detergent aisle at the grocery store and buy Tide, because "Tide makes me feel like I'm a good mom." "It makes me feel like I can take care of my family and I know my clothes will come out clean." "Tide is special, and my family deserves it."

At every step, we want to use words and marketing strategies that reflect our differentiation. What is your brand and how are you special? What are you passionate about? What makes you different from the person sitting next to you? You could be sitting next to someone with the same skill set, almost identical education and training, the same hair color and even the same set of contacts. What makes you different? You must clearly communicate, through everything you do, why you are the ideal choice and make yourself relevant to that target audience.

Second, what makes you compelling? Why should I (your target audience) care about this uniqueness? You (and your mother) might think you are the greatest asset any company could hope to employ. But personal branding is not all about you. It's about the needs, interests and goals of the audience you are targeting. You need to make sure the message you deliver to that audience is compelling and clearly articulates why they should care. Think about my example of the two interior designers. The one I find compelling is the one who ensures that I (her target client) recognize the unique skills and traits she brings to the engagement. She makes sure that I see her flair (by how she dresses, her marketing materials and her language) and her outgoing personality and that I feel reassured as I ask questions during the interview. She makes sure I find her relevant.

Then, you need to demonstrate that you are credible. Credibility and integrity are not traits you can promote just by saying, "My personal brand is that of trust!" Credibility and integrity are intangible; they are experienced, proven, tested and consistent. They are the values our "fans" will refer to as they sing our praises, refer us to prospects and nominate us for recognition.

The only formula I know for building credibility within a personal brand is a pretty simple one. It starts with articulating your values: telling people what you stand for, what matters to you, what you will fight for. And it ends with being consistent (the fourth C!) with the values and beliefs you advocate. By doing so, you build a reputation of integrity. This is what we mean by "walking the talk." My new interior designer will ensure that when I see her website, talk to her former clients, read her blog and begin working with her, the traits and values she conveyed in our first meeting are consistent across all her other points of marketing.

Here's an example: Let's say you are passionate about transparency. You believe people should see you for what you are. "What you see (with me) is what you get," you say. It is vitally important to you that people learn to trust that you are a man of your word, that there are no "smoke and mirrors," that you are what you say.

What happens if I go to your website and I see you representing yourself differently? Or if I see you interviewed at a company "town hall" meeting and you recite rehearsed words fed to you by your public relations team? Maybe I repeatedly overhear you speaking ill of another colleague or competitor. Is that the behavior of someone who is transparent? I don't think so.

I need to know that if your values involve qualities such as being approachable, warm and inviting, then I can walk into your office if I need something and you're not going to shut the door in my face. I need to know that if I leave you a message, you're going to call me back. I need to know that if I have an issue I need to talk to you about, you'll make time for me. Consistency is critical. Otherwise, I'll see your values as just lip service, "spin" or "fluff." When we talk about credibility and integrity, we're talking about acting according to your values. It's the walk-the-talk philosophy. Through repetitive consistency, I believe what you tell me and show me to be true. I begin to trust you.

If you develop a personal brand that is clear, compelling, credible and consistent, you will be rewarded with benefits, opportunities and the reputation you desire.

The A.... Authenticity is at the heart of your personal brand

The work that I do is all rooted in authenticity, that deep-down, quiet truism about you as a dynamic and special person that makes you unlike anyone else. It is your genuine spirit, the you that is the most real. To be in touch with your authenticity means you see yourself as a whole—the good and the bad, the successes and the failures—and you own it all. You have humility in knowing what your limitations are and where your passions stem from. To be living an authentic personal brand is to be the most empowered person you can possibly be. To be authentic is to live a life where you (the real you) are always present.

My work with executives, leaders, experts, professionals and even corporations always starts by understanding and then developing what makes them genuine. Authenticity is at the truest core of what we do in marketing our value to others.

4

Articulating your current brand

Think about your current brand. What drives you? What sets you apart from the person sitting next to you? What makes you special? This level of introspection, of self-delving, is not easy for anybody, especially since personal branding is often counterintuitive to how we were raised.

As children, we were told to blend in, not to make waves and not to call attention to ourselves. We were told just to fit in with the others. This is especially true for women. Magazines, TV shows, how-to books and gurus constantly encourage us to look and act like everyone else who is "successful" or "accomplished." We're not taught to think about what makes us special and unique. We're not taught to self-promote and boast.

But it's essential to understand what you offer the world that is unique from what others offer if you are going to be successful in business and in life. You need to take responsibility and accountability for projecting and demonstrating your value if you expect to get the benefits of a powerful reputation.

Start by thinking about what drives you. You might note, "I enjoy being around people"; "I love the thrill of the chase"; "I'm passionate about figuring out problems and bringing solutions no one else could see"; or "I've received a lot of feedback that says I'm a really good listener." Those might be the qualities you begin with to understand your current brand.

Next, consider five key words that describe you. Think beyond the obvious ones—ethical, trustworthy, hard working and loyal—because most of your competitors are saying those same things. Dig deep to understand what key words describe you, not your neighbor. This is certainly an exercise you can come back to, but getting those five current brand words is very important.

Another way you can learn more about your current personal brand is to compare your brand to others'. What brands do you feel a similarity, or affinity, with? For instance, you might say, "Harry Winston jewelry is about status and exclusivity, and so am I," or "Mercedes is elegant and forward-thinking, and so am I," or "Wal-Mart is about being friendly, approachable, easy to experience and full of value, and so am I." Spend a moment and think about some brands that you particularly relate to and what qualities, characteristics and traits in yourself align with those brands.

Was this a difficult exercise for you or an easy one? For some people, the descriptive words just roll off the tips of their tongues. They have a clear sense of what differentiates them. For others, it's tough to get to five key words. Whether this was easy or difficult, your key words become a part of how you will project and articulate your value, so it is important to keep working on them until you feel they are right. Remember, too, that personal branding is a journey, and it takes time and practice to build momentum.

KEY TAKEAWAYS

- Your current brand is how you see yourself, how you are and how others perceive you.

- To help understand your current brand:
    * Think about what drives you.
    * Determine five key words or qualities that describe you.
    * Compare yourself to other brands you admire and relate to and

determine which qualities in you align with those brands.

* Understand what you offer the world that is unique from what others offer.

5

Articulating your desired brand

Now that we have an idea of what your current brand is, we need to think about your desired brand. For some of you, your current brand is exactly what you want people to be thinking about you. In that case, you may simply need to get more creative on how you market yourself to remain relevant and compelling. For others, though, your current brand and what you want to be known for don't match. In those cases, we really need to think about and identify a desired brand—your legacy.

Let's start with a few questions about you. Think about how you would like others to see you and feel about you, and answer these questions:

- **If you were a car, what kind of car would you want to be?** Would you be a sexy sports car? Would you be a high-powered big truck? Would you be a family passenger van? What type of car would you want to be and why?

- **If you were a song, what kind of song would you want to be?** Would you want to be a classic melody or a fast–paced, aggressive, heavy metal number? Would there be words in your song, or would it just be melody?

- **If you were a beverage, what kind of beverage would you want to be?** Would you be an energy drink? Would you be a fancy

Starbucks drink? Would you be an alcoholic beverage? Would you be a kid's juice drink?

These questions are fun and whimsical, but they're also important in giving you a sense of how you would like to project yourself. Are you a fast racecar, high-energy-drink-type person? Do you see yourself more as a family sedan, maybe a nonalcoholic, no caffeinated beverage that plays to a melody that's a little bit more traditional? This exercise helps you get a sense of your desired personal brand and your style.

Another way to think about your desired personal brand is to think about the end. How do you want to be remembered? Imagine we're at your funeral, and people who have loved you, worked with you and known you casually surround us. What would you like these people to say about the difference you made? How do you want them to remember you? What emotions do you want them to experience as they remember your life and contribution? You might want them to say things such as:

"She gave one hundred percent of herself to everything she did ..."
"She made those around her feel welcomed, valued and loved ..."
"He was a great father and husband ..."
"He could always be counted on in a pinch ..."
"She was the best (fill in the blank) I ever knew ..."

Often, in working with clients, I hear them describe their current brands this way: "My current reputation is based on producing financial impact to the bottom line of the firm and quarterly improvements that meet expectations of internal and external stakeholders ..." Then, when we get to their desired brand and this exercise, they get quiet. They say they want to be known as "a good dad." Or I hear something such as, "You know, I want my staff to feel like I was always there for them, that I always had their backs." All of a sudden, we start to hear authentic emotional qualities. Remember that branding is about emotions.

When you look over the list of things that you want to be remembered for, I encourage you to really focus in on the emotional words, the ones that create feelings rather than words that are tactical or strategic or have dollar amounts tied to them.

Now, take those words, feelings and thoughts and write five key words that reflect your desired brand. They may be the same five words that you wrote for your current brand, or they might be different. How do you want to be remembered?

Just as before, this may not be easy. We're getting really close to figuring out your personal brand: what makes you unique and what strengths you have. You might already be seeing some patterns jump off the page!

KEY TAKEAWAYS

- Your desired brand is the legacy you hope to leave after you pass. This legacy is set in your reputation and the connections and experiences others had with you when you were alive.

- To help determine your desired brand:
  * Think of five key words that reflect how you want people to see you.
  * Think of how you want people to remember you and feel about you after you are gone.
  * Formulate your thoughts in terms of feelings and emotions, rather than words that are tactical or have dollar amounts tied to them. Branding is about emotions and feelings.

6

Soliciting feedback

Think about your current brand and your desired brand. How close are the two? Do you really know? The best way to assess how close you are to your desired reputation is with honest and reliable feedback.

Let's look at it this way: Have you ever been sitting across the desk from your boss as he begins to share some of the concerns and feelings your peers have about you? Some of them find you difficult to deal with. Others have commented that you take over meetings. Or maybe your staff feels you don't have their backs and advocate for their needs. As we learn, especially at times like these, we don't always know what others think of us.

My good friend Olivia (not her real name) had been promoted to senior vice president of a large international company. She was in charge of a national sales team and had been hired in October. In December, the company hosted a holiday party, and her team flew in from across the country to celebrate. For the first time, she met several of the people on her national team in person. Halfway into the party, she walked into the restroom, shut the stall door behind her and heard two women come in right after her. The first woman said to the second, "Have you met Olivia Owens?"

Hearing her name mentioned, my friend perked up. She thought, "Oh my gosh, I'm going to hear a conversation about me!"

Then the second woman replied to the first, "Yes! I have met Olivia! Who the heck does she think she is?"

Olivia was stunned. As she describes it, she wanted to curl up on the floor and become invisible. She continued to overhear, unbeknownst to her colleagues, a conversation between two executives on her team describing someone they perceived as "stubborn, arrogant, pushy and exclusive."

But that's not Olivia! Olivia knows herself to be collaborative, engaging, supportive and, yes, driven—but in a good way.

Similarly, I worked with an attorney who should have been on track to become a partner in the firm. However, she repeatedly heard feedback from her colleagues and superiors that she wasn't seen as a "team player." This was frustrating to her, because it kept limiting her opportunities for advancement in the firm. She wasn't included in the partner retreat, and she wasn't invited to happy hour with the other partners, which was typically what they did when they were grooming somebody for a partnership.

We talked about this "team player" feedback. To her, the term team player meant something very different from what it meant to her peers. To her, being a team player meant sitting her team down around a table and saying, "You do this, you do this, you do this and you do this." That was how she saw team play—clear, direct and highly functional. The firm had a different vision. The more she perpetuated this behavior and reinforced this reputation, the more limiting it became.

Feedback is an important tool to measure, assess and test reality against perception. It helps us gauge whether we're close to our desired brand. Many of my clients discover through feedback that their current brand is perceived to be closer to their desired brand than they thought. What a discovery!

Other clients learn of positive traits others see in them that they didn't realize they were bringing to the table. What a gift that knowledge would be!

I have a client, for example, who is a successful female entrepreneur in a high profile but heavily bureaucratic industry. She is also very tall, with striking, naturally red hair. In her mind, her stature and appearance were liabilities since, as she put it, "My look makes an entrance into a room before I do!" However, after receiving personal branding feedback, we learned that her target audiences loved her bold appearance and attributed the impact and success of her message to the forcefulness of her physical presence. She was seen as more passionate, credible and confident because of this striking appearance. Upon learning this, we were able to weave her appearance into her personal brand marketing strategy in a more direct way. She now feels comfortable leveraging this personal strength more intentionally.

Positive feedback is always welcome. But negative feedback, like the kind Olivia encountered, is just as useful. Imagine you accidentally overheard gossip that reflected negative feelings about you. Maybe you overheard two colleagues complaining about the way you manage meetings or your lack of participation in team activities. What powerful feedback! What a gift! They have alerted you to a perception brewing, and that perception can spread and grow if you don't take action.

How to solicit feedback

There are many forms of feedback. In some companies, employees have regular performance reviews and evaluations. Typically, they fit into a structured format, dictated by the human resources team. Maybe you have participated in formal employee performance or communications surveys or evaluations, moderated by a professional coach who is certified to conduct this survey. These tools can be used to assess everything from brand to communication style to a multitude of different personal insights. All these methods can offer valuable feedback and perspective. There are also informal forms of feedback, and we all have access to these. We can have hallway conversations with colleagues or associates. We can take clients out to lunch and ask them about our perceived brand. I just mentioned that gossip could be another form of feedback. I'm not advocating that you pay attention to all water-cooler conversation, but if you overhear gossip, maybe you can spot a pattern in your perceived behavior and detect important insights about your brand. Maybe you can identify roadblocks in your career or relationships that are a result of this perception.

In assessing your personal brand, I encourage you to consider feedback from colleagues, peers, clients (even past clients), staff, direct reports and associates. Ask yourself: Who do I need to bring in close? Who do I need to get feedback from? Who will give me honest, compelling, relevant information that will allow me to become more effective in building my reputation?

Encouraging honest feedback: Building trust
It isn't always easy to get this kind of input. We often need to encourage feedback, because people withhold it for many reasons. Sometimes, people don't give us their honest opinions because they're afraid they will upset the apple cart, or maybe they don't want to hurt our feelings. Sometimes, they're not sure or confident about their input, or maybe they want to avoid conflict. Sometimes, they simply haven't been asked for their feedback.

Offering honest feedback can be as painful for the person giving it as it can be for you to hear it. To feel safe in offering feedback, it's important that the people you approach feel respected and valued and see you as open, trustworthy and receptive. Respondents need to know that their feedback is welcome and will help you grow. If they don't feel safe offering feedback, they may be reluctant or make comments that aren't honest. If you don't get candid feedback from your sources, it affects your ability to make good decisions. You can miss important opportunities because you will be basing decisions on suspect information. If you don't get honest feedback, it can lead to brand incompetence and misperception.

When soliciting feedback, keep in mind that you receive respect by showing respect. No matter how painful the feedback may feel or how opportunistic you perceive it to be, you need to show appreciation for the input. Somebody took the time to open up his heart and give you feedback that is potentially a gold mine. (Consider how you've felt if you've ever been asked to give feedback that was uncomfortable or painful. You took a chance and opened yourself to another's potential anger. If your feedback is met with disrespect and rage, you are less likely to be forthcoming the next time. Similarly, if the feedback is received in the spirit in which it was offered—to be helpful—then you feel respected and inclined to help again.)

At LIDA360 we developed a proprietary feedback tool to assess personal brands. When we issue this feedback tool for clients, we remind them that when receiving feedback, no matter how positive or negative, the most important response is "thank you." The only way to gain trust and get honest feedback is to treat those who provide feedback—positive or negative—equally. The moment you start rebutting the validity of the feedback—defending your position and perception of yourself—is the moment you begin to destroy trust. We also remind clients to pay attention to the expression on their faces, because even if they're controlling their language and their bodies, their faces tell it all. Remember that people are giving you feedback—it's a gift.

Despite our best efforts to solicit honest feedback, we won't always be successful. In those cases it can be appropriate to solicit anonymous feedback, such as with a survey. Many online tools are available where you can see responses in aggregate unattributed (no names attached to responses). Or, you can hire somebody to conduct the feedback portion who can feed it back to you unattributed, so you see the responses but not who said what. Anonymous feedback is helpful if you feel that your audience may not be wiling to share comments unless those comments are confidential.

How to read feedback

When you get feedback that isn't anonymous, watch for nonverbal as well as verbal clues that the person offering the feedback is not being completely honest with you. He may not be doing this intentionally; sometimes offering feedback is uncomfortable. You want to pay attention to warning signs, such as a change in vocal tonality. Have you ever had a difficult conversation with someone and suddenly her voice got really high? Halting words might also signal a problem: Is the message really difficult for her to articulate? Is there a reason she can't get the words out?

What about ambiguous messages? We often hear the statement "there's truth in jest." What if somebody all of a sudden starts injecting a lot of humor to deflect and defer?

When receiving feedback, also be on the lookout for a sudden change in language usage. My default behavior, when I'm sending a direct message to my children, is to use their formal names and choose my words very carefully. If the person you're talking to begins choosing very professional language in the discussion, this could be a warning sign that he is struggling to tell you something difficult or possibly trying to cover something up.

Similarly, you should pay attention to whether someone's words match his body language. For example, say your boss is sharing positive feedback with you on the recent presentation you gave at the board meeting. As he's talking to you, his posture becomes defensive—he crosses his arms, avoids eye contact, perhaps he starts fidgeting with a pen or his hair. Your boss could be struggling with his message, and it would be a missed opportunity to hear only the positive words without noticing that he is also trying to tell you something negative, and potentially helpful.

In addition to these concerns, you need to pay close attention to how you are listening to the feedback. Often, we don't hear feedback because we're thinking ahead. Research has shown that when we're thinking ahead, we're missing what the person is saying. As somebody is talking to you, you might be thinking, "Uh-huh, uh-huh, I get it. I got it. I know where you're going, and so I'm already there." However, you might end up coming to a wrong conclusion and miss the opportunity to learn something important and helpful.

Likewise, we often use emotional filters to hear feedback, which can be limiting. We all have emotional filters, predisposed ways of seeing and judging incoming information. We all have preferences, prejudices or biases to certain people, communication styles, tonality or body language. We use those beliefs and emotional filters to judge and create a story around what somebody's trying to tell us. For example, if we believe that "all teenagers exaggerate" or "women talk too much," then our receipt of their information will be clouded, and we could miss important clues. While emotional filters are often our mind's way of being efficient, they can inhibit our ability to listen and hear feedback in its truest form.

Often, we don't listen well because we're striving for our own validation. We're looking for confirmation of our expertise or our beliefs, and we're not hearing what the other person is saying. We're looking for ways their message supports what we believe to be true.

Another reason we might not hear the content of the feedback is because we're protecting ourselves. Our defense mechanisms kick in—we bat down feedback that we perceive to be harsh, critical and painful—because we want to protect ourselves. While this type of reaction is helpful in self-preservation, it's not useful from a personal branding process standpoint: We may miss gems that would help us move toward our desired reputation.

Finally, there's a lot of noise in the world today that can get in the way of our ability to listen constructively to feedback. Between the Internet, cell phones and busier-than-ever lives, we're easily distracted. This can have a direct impact on the way we receive feedback. We stand no real chance of truly hearing and understanding what somebody's trying to tell us if we're distracted.

Intent is irrelevant
In receiving and evaluating feedback, you might be inclined to conjecture ideas around the intent or motive of the respondent. Perhaps you're thinking they have an ax to grind or an agenda to promote. Maybe you think they could be trying to steer you in a bad direction. Regardless of how you interpret their feedback, intent doesn't have a lot of relevance. We can't possibly know what someone intends (or is thinking), and second-guessing only diminishes the value of the feedback.

Receiving disrespectful feedback
Disrespect is inappropriate, unfair criticism. For example, it's fair for someone to tell you "I believe you take over meetings" but not to tell you, "You should sit in the back of the room and shut up!" You should never be put in a position in which the feedback you receive causes you to feel like a doormat. If you have asked for genuine feedback from someone and he offers disrespectful, unconstructive criticism, a response from you might be, "I appreciate your input. I'm not sure I agree, but I will certainly give it consideration." This could diffuse a volatile situation and might cause the respondent to reconsider the negativity of his comments going forward.

Think about the kind of feedback you need
At this point, you can start crafting your own feedback game plan. Think about the type of feedback you want to solicit and whether it's business or personal. What feedback on your brand do you think you need at this point? Maybe you're trying to gauge if your current brand is close to your desired brand. Maybe you're trying to find out what your brand looks like to others.

What feedback are you looking to solicit at work and in your personal life? Here are some simple brand evaluation questions you could email to eight or ten of your clients, peers, colleagues and maybe even some staff:

"Do I have a personal brand, and if so, what is that brand?"
"If you referred me to someone, how would you introduce me?"
"When you think of me, what special traits do you believe I have?"

Questions like these assess perception: What are you known for? What is your reputation?

Whenever I receive a referral, the first question I ask is, "What were you told about me?" It is important to me to understand how I am perceived in the marketplace. What are people saying about my brand? How are they introducing me? The question, "Would you refer me to somebody else, and if so, how would you introduce me?" provides critical insight into your brand.

Asking "What do you see as my competitive advantage?" might uncover strengths you didn't know you had. Then follow up with the question: "How do you know that? What do I do that makes you say that?" You are not asking someone to tell you if you are a valuable person. Rather, you want to know if she believes you have the ability to build credibility for a competitive advantage and how she would differentiate you. This helps you gauge the distance between your current and desired brands.

Once you have solicited feedback from others, be sure to keep them in the loop. Let them know you are on a personal brand journey and touch base with them in six months or a year. Let them know about your progress and what you're doing to effect positive change. Thank them for their insight.

Personal branding is not about changing who you are

This personal branding journey you're on is not about changing you, and it's not about changing other people. You can influence, you can affect, you can even manipulate other people, but you can't literally change them.

It's important to understand what you actually have control over. This graphic helps us understand many things about control. At the center of the circle is where you are. You are set there. You cannot unwind or undo everything that has ever happened to you before you began reading this information. Your DNA, experiences, opportunities, challenges and gifts are all set at

the moment you began this personal branding journey. That's all in the past. Neither you nor I can go back and change them. Likewise, the outer circle represents the world that, like you, can't change how it is wired. You can't change other people, nor can you change the way the world is.

What you can control and affect is the band in the middle, which is your behavior. Where you interact with the world, where you come into contact with other people is where perception is formed. The more times you act a certain way, the more often the world—other people—will form perceptions about you based on how they feel about that behavior.

You might receive feedback that causes you to think, "I'm hearing that I'm not a team player" or, "I'm getting feedback that says I'm not approachable." These are perceptions you can change through your behavior. One of the changes you might make if you are getting that feedback would be to leave your office door open more often. Or you might look at your personal style: Do you appear closed off and distant? Maybe you dress more formally than the rest of your team and colleagues. You might look at the way you are communicating with your staff. Are you using overly formal language, or do they see your casual side, too?

I met a woman in one of my programs who was probably in her early twenties. She came up to me after my presentation and said, "I've got this brand at work as 'the office mom.' Everybody calls me the office mom, and I get feedback that I'm valued because I'm the office mom." But she continued, "I'm getting passed up for promotions. I don't even think I'm getting any respect, because I have this brand, this label." Being known as "the office mom" was clearly hindering her opportunities.

We talked about what she had been doing to build that reputation. In fact, she'd been feeding right into it! She was the person who organized the Friday afternoon parties. She was the one who always set up the meetings with the napkins and the coffee pot and the bottled waters. She was the one who cleaned up afterwards. She was the one who made sure everybody got a birthday card on his or her birthday. She was a very giving, generous, warm person, but because she was feeding into this perception, she was limiting her opportunities. So she had to pull back. It didn't mean she went from being a warm, generous, approachable person to being cold and distant. She didn't change her identity or ignore the experiences in her past that led her to want to be so giving. But she had to remove that brand perception because otherwise, she was not going to be taken seriously and advance in the organization.

Similarly, the female attorney who was not considered a "team player" re-evaluated her behavior to make a positive change and attract her desired opportunities. We developed concrete actions she could use to promote her brand assets and changed the way she interacted with her team and colleagues. For instance, she didn't always speak up at meetings; she let other people have the spotlight. She began asking more questions rather than offering answers. We used her feedback to guide her behavior and build up her reputation and credibility within the firm. She eventually did make partner, because the partners saw her as more apt to be a team player and to be moving in a direction that would grow the firm, her staff and the values of the firm.

As you craft your feedback strategy, consider the areas that you'll act on as they align with your values. I'm not going to change who I am; I'm not going to change my beliefs; I can't change my DNA; and I'm not going to change my values or those qualities that make me authentic. But I am going to make changes in my behavior to get closer to my desired brand. As I craft and communicate my personal brand, my objective is to create consistent messaging that's compelling and unique to the audiences who can assign me value and provide me with opportunity.

KEY TAKEAWAYS

- Feedback is always a gift. Because your goal is to move from your current reputation toward your desired brand, you need feedback to gauge how far you are from your desired brand.

- The intent of the speaker doesn't have relevance when it comes to receiving feedback, because we can't possibly know what others intend.

- Personal branding involves making changes based on the feedback you receive to get you closer to your desired brand; it does not mean changing who you are.

- Always show appreciation for feedback. This will keep the flow of information coming to you.

- Solicit feedback on your personal brand by asking people you trust, "Do I have a personal brand, and if so, what is it?" Or "When you think of me, what special traits do you think I possess?" Look for patterns in the responses.

- When receiving feedback, pay attention to both the verbal and nonverbal cues of the people offering it. Look for signs that what they are saying might not be consistent with what they mean, such as:
  * Change of vocal tonality
  * Halting words
  * Sudden change in language usage
  * Words not matching body language

- Avoid these common roadblocks when receiving feedback:
  * Not paying attention and thinking ahead, instead of actually listening to what the person is saying
  * Putting the feedback through an emotional filter
  * Striving for your own validation
  * Getting defensive
  * Letting modern distractions, such as cell phones, interfere with your ability to hear what's being said

7

Writing your brand promise

The next step is for you to write your brand promise. A brand promise is not a marketing statement; it's not a tag line, and it's not a slogan. It's a very personal statement that will help guide you through living your personal brand with intention and move you in the direction of your desired personal brand. Your efforts toward target audiences, image, marketing identity and online branding will all filter through your brand promise.

Your brand promise should look something like this: "In order to be known for (your desired brand qualities,) I will hold myself out to others in this way: (your behavior, actions, attitude); and I will demonstrate authenticity in this way: (how you will let people see you as real, genuine). I will know my brand promise is working when I see this: (benefits, goals you hope to achieve).

We'll approach this in steps, starting with "in order to be known for..." This is where you'll write your desired brand. As we discussed in Chapter 5, here is you write what you want to be known for. Ultimately, what is the reputation you're creating for yourself?

Once you've done that, think about how you will hold yourself out to others. If you are a human resources professional and your desired brand is to be known as approachable, warm and compassionate, how will you act on the job? Will you keep your door open? Will you make good eye contact? Will you work on your body language and make sure that your desk is clear so that employees feel you're approachable? How will you show up so that you can continue to build toward your desired brand?

Similarly, how will you demonstrate your authentic, genuine self to draw others to you? Using the example of the HR professional, if you want to be known as approachable and trustworthy, you might demonstrate authenticity by sharing some of your personal stories to make yourself relatable. You might place framed photos of your family in your office so colleagues and staff can learn more about your personal life. You might share stories of your own attempts at career advancement and how they worked out for you. Those might be ways that you can show people who you really are.

Your brand promise is a critical piece of your personal brand development. I encourage you to continually spend time on this. Let it evolve. As you live and work through the promise of how you will be, your identity will begin to flourish. Your personal brand will become the filter through which you will make decisions.

Your brand promise may work itself into some kind of a tag line. It may become the vision statement for your company. It may help you clarify why you love the type of work that you do or the company that you work for.

I've had clients turn their brand promises into their computer screen saver (for example, "Always treat others with respect and kindness"). One of my clients wrote hers —"I will strive for inclusivity and collaboration and will not hold onto information or beliefs if they can benefit others"— on an index card and taped it to the steering wheel in her car so that every time she was going to a meeting or out and about, she reminded herself, "This is what I'm working toward, and this is how I need to show up. I need to constantly remind myself what I'm striving for. My brand is a gift."

KEY TAKEAWAYS

- Your brand promise is not a marketing slogan. It is a very personal statement of identity and belief.

- A brand promise will help guide you to live your personal brand with intention and move you toward your desired brand.

- A brand promise includes the following pieces:
  * Your desired brand qualities
  * The behavior, actions and attitudes you intend to display in carrying out your brand promise
  * The ways you will let people see you as real, genuine and authentic
  * The benefits and goals you hope to achieve

8

Understanding your target audience

Knowing which audiences you should target is critical to marketing an effective personal brand. You can't be relevant to everyone out there. Not every potential client, vendor, teammate or employee will love you.

Your focus will be on the ones who do need to find you relevant and compelling. These are the clients, colleagues, employees, peers and readers who can offer you opportunities or things of value or advance your career. These are the audiences that need to experience and appreciate your value.

Let's start with some questions:

- Have you ever been part of a group or team and felt like nobody understood you and you didn't fit in, that the people you were with didn't get your jokes, find your talents important or appreciate your contributions?

- Have you ever felt outside of every conversation?

- Have you ever gotten home and realized that you act completely differently at home—more like your true self? I've had jobs where I literally couldn't wait to take off what I felt was the costume that I'd been wearing all day.

Often we are not clicking with the audiences that we try to align ourselves with, and we feel out of sorts. Most likely your job complements your personal values, because there's a reason you chose to do the type of work you do, and there's a reason you chose the company that you work for. But if your personal brand conflicts with the values of the organization you work for, that could be why your stomach has been hurting. Whether your work is in the area of environmental sustainability, health care or interior design, it's important that your personal brand support that effort, or it will reveal a big disconnect. When your values, competencies and goals are not supported or in line with those of the people you work with, you feel misaligned.

Let's go back for a minute to the questions I posed earlier, now addressed to your target audience:

- If your target audience were a car, what kind of car would it be?

- If it were a song, what kind of song would your audience be and why?

- Finally, what kind of beverage would it be? Would it be a nice, chilled chardonnay or an energy drink? Would it be a cold glass of milk? Why?

Look back at where I asked you those questions about yourself—If you were a car, what kind of car would you be? If you were a song, what kind of song would you be? If you were a beverage, what kind of beverage would you be and why?—and match your answers there against how you answered these questions about your target audiences.

Ideally, the answers will be the same or very similar. I might see myself as a BMW, and my client would be a Lexus. I would be a hard rock song, and my client would be heavy metal. I would be an energy drink, and my client would be a strong cup of coffee.

We should target the audience that finds us relevant: the audience that gets our jokes, appreciates our uniqueness and embraces and values what makes us special. Your target audience is looking for you, and I can tell you through years of experience that when you find that sweet spot—when you locate the audience that will find you relevant and compelling— things will fall into place! Your marketing will become a lot less energy-intensive and a lot less costly. You will go from shotgun to laser marketing.

Remember, the way you build credibility with your target audience is to articulate your values and act consistently. Imagine how much work it would take if you were focused on having credibility with everyone you came across. However, if you focus on the audience that needs to find you relevant and build credibility with them, they in turn will assign you opportunity and value. We want to be sure we're focusing our efforts on the right people.

Consider, for example, a brand of automobile that we're all familiar with: Volvo. Volvo makes us feel safe. I've done an exercise in front of very, very large groups in which I ask everyone to shout out the name of a car that equals "safety" in their minds. Everyone yells, "Volvo!" Most of us have never been in an accident in a Volvo, yet in our minds that brand equals safety. Volvo intentionally markets that brand to audiences that are attracted to the safety message and will find it relevant. Volvo doesn't invest time and money marketing to teenagers or risk-takers that couldn't care less about safety. They market the safety message to mothers and fathers, to families, to people who may have survived an accident. To these people, safety is important.

Researching your audience
Once you've defined your target audience, it's important to understand everything you can about who they are and what they like, because your goal is to show yourself as relevant to solving their problems or meeting their needs. If you don't know much about them, they might all blur together in your mind and appear all the same. Or, you risk trying to

appeal to them in ways they can't understand.

I worked with a client in California who was in the financial planning profession, and she was passionate about technology. She was in her late twenties, a very bright young woman who loved all things technical. She managed all her appointment data through her iPhone; she emailed seminar invitations; she emailed client newsletters, alerts and feedback surveys; she utilized technology in the most robust ways possible. She invested a lot of time and energy into understanding her field, developing her skills and using technology to communicate her value to clients and prospects.

Interestingly, however, her target audience was composed of couples currently in retirement. These weren't people in their forties or even fifties. They were mostly seniors in their sixties, seventies and beyond. That was her sweet spot, and she heavily relied on technology to communicate with and market to them.

The "open rates" on her emails were terrible; her feedback surveys came back with hardly any responses. Her marketing wasn't reaching its target, and it was obvious she hadn't studied her audience, which wasn't comfortable with technology. They were terrified to close their computers at night because they were afraid all their information would be gone in the morning. She was using the wrong marketing to get to the right audience. Once she better understood her audience and started doing more traditional marketing—phone calls, stopping by, direct mail—her client response rates and engagements skyrocketed.

In doing the "car, song, beverage" exercise, one of my clients said if he were a car, he would be a NASCAR racecar. He would be built for one time around the track; he would be all about speed—few gears, all about action! If he were a song, he would be heavy metal. If he were a beverage, he would be the highest-octane energy drink you could imagine. Then we began narrowing his target audience, and he told me that his audience would be an old Volkswagen bug from the 1960s with the big flower stickers on it. If his audience were a song, it would be a classic American pop song. If it were a beverage, he said it would be milk. Seriously! Those were his answers! You can see where there might be some confusion and misalignment in how he relates to his audience.

This man began to realize that he needed to change some of his behavior to communicate the values of his brand, because he and his audiences were speaking different languages and living different styles. He began taking slower strides when walking into a room to meet these clients. He talked more slowly to ensure they heard every word. He leveraged his energy and passion in ways that his audience could relate to (e.g., he spoke about their common mission, engaging this audience in the cause), not in ways that would cause them to recoil. Just because his audience was not aligned in behavior to him did not mean he needed to find another audience or reinvent himself to be relevant. He was in control of how his behavior influenced and affected that audience, and he made the choice to modify his behavior to be more approachable to and engaged with this target group. Making such a choice is always in your control; it is your option.

Study the members of your target audience carefully. Do they embrace technology? Do they seek efficiency, or do they want to have intimate conversations? Do they want you to drop by, have a cup of tea and sit and talk? You need to make sure that you're responding to your audience's needs. What do they want, and what will motivate them? Who else is influencing this audience? Are they active in social media? Are there groups they participate in?

Understand the demographics of your targets. Do they live in a specific region? Are they of a certain age or generation? Today, there are very distinct generational gaps between the 79 million baby boomers in the U.S. and the millennial genterations coming behind them. Demographics play a huge role in how we brand ourselves and how we create relevancy and a compelling message to a target audience. It's not a one-size-fits-all world.

Through surveys and feedback, assess what motivates and influences your audience. You can easily find a lot of information online, done by others who may be targeting your same audience. If you're looking to target the millennial generation, for instance, there are numerous papers, books and other tools to help you gain understanding about that audience.

Don't forget to research where your target audience hangs out, as well. Are they active online? What type of groups do they belong to? Do they hang out in industry associations? This will help you once you begin your marketing efforts.

Pay attention to your audience's functional and emotional needs
As you research and identify your audience, it is important that you concentrate on more than their functional needs. Most of us are really good at knowing the functional needs of our audience, the requirements that make us even a distinct possibility to them. If you've ever been a hiring manager, for example, you look at a resume to make sure the candidates have the required skills, core competences, right amount of education, right amount of years of work experience—all the areas where you can check the boxes and make sure that they fit. Functional needs are the basics. You will often find functional needs spelled out in Requests for Proposals (RFPs) and on job descriptions.

Many of us focus on meeting our audience's functional needs by producing resumes and using lists of bullet points on business cards and brochures. If your audience needs business development, sales, real estate representation, advertising exposure or market research, these are the ways you clearly articulate that you know how to do this. These are things an audience needs to check off before you're even part of the conversation. If you don't meet these needs, there's no use going forward.

But if you only address these functional needs, you will find yourself at a great disadvantage. Audiences also have emotional needs, and these are just as important as their functional needs.

A hiring manager, for example, will assess whether he feels a candidate will be a good team player and fit in with the group. Is she someone the staff would enjoy working with? Will he make me feel good about my decision to hire him?

Starbucks coffee shops meet my functional needs if I crave a warm beverage, need a snack or would like a place to get some caffeine. What Starbucks does even better, however, is consider the needs of its ideal target audience and create an emotional experience as well: I go to Starbucks because I feel a sense of warmth and community. The surroundings are pleasant and welcoming. The barista knows my drink and greets me when I enter the store.

Starbucks has done a beautiful job of hitting the emotional qualities that its audience is looking for. When you walk into a Starbucks, the employees interact with you and make conversation. You find comfortable chairs to relax in and people who have spent part of their day enjoying Starbucks. People who aren't attracted to Starbucks aren't attracted to those emotional benefits. But millions of others find this irresistible.

When you think about the emotional needs of your audience, ask yourself: What does my audience need to feel from me? Does my target audience need to feel that they're going to be treated as if they are special? Will they be attended to and cared for as valued clients? For instance, maybe you are a photographer who specializes in personal branding. You might describe the benefits that your audience gets from you as: "Not only do I take an attractive, high-resolution photograph of you, but I also take time to make sure that your true character comes forward. Your brand will be revealed in the images that I reflect back to you." Those are real benefits! You're hitting the functional and the emotional needs of your audience. When I hire someone who has an expertise in personal branding to take my picture, I'm expecting more than a passport photo, so he needs to communicate the benefits that I'm getting from him.

If you can meet the emotional needs of your audience, you can create market "stickiness," brand attraction and equity. When you talk to prospective clients, you have to focus on the tactical—you look at the anticipated outcomes and the deliverables. However, you also have to acknowledge that your clients need confirmation, validation and empathy. They may need empowerment and motivation. They may need to feel that they can trust your recommendations and be confident in your advice and counsel.

Your competitors might be good at producing many of the tangible, functional things your audience needs. But your value proposition— your unique talent— lies in your ability and intuitiveness in meeting your clients' emotional needs as well. This gives you a competitive advantage.

Identify who is influencing your audience
As you consider the needs of your audience members, also pay attention to who is influencing them. For instance, if your target audience is your direct supervisor, consider who is influencing her. In this case, your peers in the company or team, your direct staff or even trade publications could be impacting your boss. If so, you need to be relevant to these entities, too, as they can help you build your reputation (your personal brand) with your supervisor. If it's important to your boss that you build your brand position as an expert in your field and you know your boss is active in a particular association, for instance, you might choose to write an article highlighting your expertise in that association's magazine. This will raise your profile in business circles and, perhaps even more important, in your boss' eyes.

Let's say your audiences are clients and prospects. Who's influencing them? The media (print, broadcast and online)? If so, you will need to promote your brand through these outlets. Your staff? If this is the case, the way that your staff members interact with your clients is going to support or refute your brand credibility and influence your clients and prospects. Your staff, company, colleagues and media presence are extensions of you and must be consistent voices that reflect your differentiation and uniqueness. How we walk the talk is what ultimately builds integrity and credibility.

KEY TAKEAWAYS

- Your target audience is the relevant group you focus on to promote your brand. You can't market yourself to everyone. Focus on the audiences who need to "get" you.

- Pay attention to the functional and emotional needs of your audience. What tangible things do they need to get from you, and what emotional connections or feelings do they need to have about you?

- Where is your audience hanging out? Where do they gather socially and professionally? Once you've found the right audience, you should get to know everything you can about them to show yourself as relevant and compelling. Become intentional about being where your audience is—in person and online.

- Pay attention to who is influencing your target audience, including colleagues, associations and media. Who has the ear and the attention of the people you want to reach?

9

Assessing your competition

We can't neglect our competitors. We have to know what they're up to. We have to understand what our competitors do well and how they're attracting the attention of our target audience. We can learn from them by taking some of their best practices and seeing if these practices feel natural and authentic to us.

As you evaluate and assess your competitors—online, in print or in person—consider these questions:

- What are they missing? Are they skipping some steps? Are they overlooking opportunities that can benefit you?

- Are they targeting the same audience as you? If they are, are they targeting it in the same way?

- Where do your competitors hang out? Who are they networking with?

- Are they finding great opportunities that, perhaps, you've been missing? What can you learn from them?

While I do not advocate branding yourself against your competitors (i.e., leveraging their weaknesses in articulating your strengths), it is important to understand what your competitors are doing. Know their weaknesses, but don't promote yourself by drawing attention to their deficits. Instead, highlight your value, show instances where you live consistently with your beliefs and enjoy the credibility you will develop.

KEY TAKEAWAYS

- Learn from your competition. Watch what they do well and emulate what feels authentic for you.

- Look for opportunities that your competition might be missing. Capitalize on those opportunities to appeal to the same target audience.

10

Tying it all together

Once you've looked at your current and desired brands and taken note of your target audience and competition, you're ready to begin crafting a strategy to make yourself relevant and compelling to that target audience.

You will look for opportunities to integrate your brand across your relationships and begin thinking about how you live online and how you can be consistent in the choices you make. You can now begin to create your own luck! One of the greatest benefits from marketing an intentional personal brand is that you attract desired opportunities. When you take control of your reputation and manage the expectation others have of you, your marketing becomes much more effective and cost efficient. This works the same for companies. When companies market through a brand, using their brand as a filter, their goals are easier to define and their decisions are easier to make because they're not relying on gut or intuition. Instead, they can rely on a metric that they've set out: This is how we want to be seen in the future, so this is what we need to do now.

Remember, personal branding is about setting the expectation others will have of you. You determine what value, contribution and reputation you want to have in the minds of your target audience. Other people have beliefs about you. It may not feel fair, but it's true. You can influence how they perceive you through your behavior and how you communicate your values.

As you craft your strategy, don't forget that you can't rely on personal branding to make you someone you aren't. Your personal brand must stem from your authentic self, your true values. This is why it is so important to understand how you want your personal brand to be known, because the marketing will be the call to action. The branding is about setting the promise of the experience.

In the coming chapters, I offer several marketing strategies and tactics for you to consider. Not all will work for you. I present them with the understanding that if they are right for you, based on your goals and desired brand, they will provide a framework and strategy for you to leverage your personal brand and stand apart from others. Through careful and focused personal branding and marketing, you will enjoy the benefits of increased visibility, recognition for your accomplishments, greater opportunity and satisfaction in your personal and professional relationships.

Before we get to the marketing piece, however, let's take a moment to recharge. The journey you are on will require passion, commitment, focus and self-confidence. Personal branding may be simple, but it is not easy. Now is a good time to remind yourself that you have been successful before. Reflect on the patterns, common traits and attributes in your past successes that might reveal the source of the strength you will draw on to begin to market your personal brand.

Articulate your superhero moment
Think back over your career, or your personal life, and remember a time when you felt like a superhero. Recall a time—and we've all had them—when you accomplished or achieved something, and at the end of that experience you felt invincible, as if you had super powers and could achieve anything! For many of us, our superhero moments come from a professional experience; for others, they come from a personal experience.

Maybe you were part of an organization, a process or an effort that made you feel so empowered and confident that there was nothing you couldn't do! Did you lead a company through a merger? Did you stop a high-stakes conversation from spinning out of control? Did you get up to speak in front of a large audience and pull it off flawlessly? Did you help a colleague with a tough situation?

This is one of the most valuable exercises we can do. I say that from a personal branding standpoint, but also from a bit of a coaching standpoint. Often we forget that we've had successes. Whatever you recalled earlier, whether it was taking your child to the bus stop for the first day of school, leading your team to financial success or standing in front of a hundred people to give a speech while you were terrified, doesn't matter. What matters is that you've had that success; you did something that perhaps challenged you, and at the end you owned the responsibility, the accountability and the outcome.

I recently worked with a woman who was a very successful business owner. When we went through this exercise, her superhero moment came in an unexpected way. She had battled breast cancer for many years, and when she was finally cleared of cancer, she ran a marathon. She had never run a marathon. In fact, she had never exercised much in her life. She set the goal of running a marathon, and she trained for it. She admits that when she finally crossed the finish line, she was the last person left in the race. Race officials had already cleaned up the little cups, taken down the signs and the scaffolding. After she finished, she said she had to be physically held up. But she had crossed the finish line! That was her superhero moment. That moment told her she could do anything she set her mind to. She expressed such energy when she talked about all that it took to overcome cancer and to cross that finish line.

In working with her, I asked, "Where is the bib number that you put on your shirt?" She told me that it was in a box with other memorabilia from that weekend. I asked her to take that bib out of storage, frame it and hang it up. It now sits in her office across from her phone. Can you imagine how confidently she handles calls when she is looking at that framed bib? It is one of the most powerful reminders of her personal success and her superhero moment.

This exercise helps us define, perhaps, how we see success for ourselves. But more important for our purposes here, it reminds us of those times when we've been to the top of the mountain, emotionally. So whatever you have pinpointed as your superhero moment, find something to remind yourself of that experience and your success. Maybe you have the trade show tag from an event that you spoke at, or maybe it was a business card from a company that you started. Whatever it is, try to find something that reminds you of your moment, and keep it front and center.

Life can get really difficult. So can tapping into your true self and authenticity. But knowing that you've had success, confidence, self-empowerment and possibilities all at your fingertips can remind you that success will come again!

KEY TAKEAWAYS

- Your personal brand gives you direction in your relationships and in the choices you make to promote yourself.

- You can gain control over your reputation and manage the expectations others have of you by being intentional and strategic about marketing your brand.

- Personal branding must integrate your authentic values and not make you into someone you are not.

- Anchoring your personal brand journey in your superhero moments—those times when you did something truly amazing, personally or professionally—is a powerful way to energize yourself.

- Keep mementos of your superhero experiences close at hand. They will remind you of the success and empowerment you've experienced in the past.

11

Your elevator pitch

There are many ways you can market your personal brand, but all the strategies rely on the same principle: You are using your desired brand as a filter for how you want to look, act and communicate with others. Each action you take, every relationship and association you make, and every way you promote yourself should confirm your desired brand.

As you begin to promote and market your personal brand, a quick and effective "elevator pitch" enables you to articulate your value proposition. Imagine this scenario: There you are, stepping into an elevator, minding your own business, when a neatly dressed professional person turns to you and asks, "So, what do you do?" Can you articulate what you do in a compelling and informative way before the elevator doors open at your floor?

In this chapter, we're talking about the elevator pitch, sometimes called an elevator speech. Wikipedia describes it as how you deliver an overview of your idea, product or service in 30 seconds or 130 words or fewer.

Often we make mistakes in our elevator pitch. We forget to say what our product or service is. We forget to say how we're relevant to the buyers or key stakeholders who should be concerned with our brand.

We forget to tell the person who's listening why she should care. You should talk about how your work relates to your brand. What makes you special?

I remember attending a very large networking event where they asked everybody in the room to give their elevator pitches. About four people in, a woman stood up and said, "I'm with Merrill Lynch, and I'm a broker," and all the people in the room responded, "Huh..." Later, another woman stood up and said, "I help couples achieve their goals and dreams and live the life they were supposed to live, and I work for Edward Jones..."

If you recognize the names of the firms they work for, you know that both women are in the financial planning field. However, they articulated their value and relevancy through very different elevator pitches. And neither of them really told me how they could be valuable to me. The first woman listed her title, and did so with a great lack of enthusiasm. She missed the opportunity to share something about herself that was interesting and compelling. The second woman created so much mystery around her service that she bored me. I did not clearly understand how she could help me. She was vague and irrelevant to me.

How to build your elevator pitch

It's important to start off your elevator pitch with a clear description of what you do. Begin your elevator pitch by telling me what you do in a succinct and easy-to-understand way. That doesn't mean reading your resume or telling me that you've practiced international trade law for fifteen years—that's what you did.

I might start off my elevator pitch by saying, "I own a national marketing and communications firm." Most people know what marketing and communications are, and by being clear, I convey: "I'm not a Subaru mechanic; I'm not a heart surgeon; I'm not a life coach; I'm not an advertising executive. I own a marketing and communications firm." That's very clear.

After you've stated what you do, then move on to explaining how you do your work differently from others in your field. Focus on something about your work or contribution that is unique, compelling and memorable. What is it about the way you work with clients that's compelling and authentic? What benefits do your clients get from working with you? What do you do for them that your competitors don't or can't?

My elevator pitch might go something like this: "I own a national marketing and communications firm, with a focus on developing strong brands." I would then add something that gives a little more clarity: "My clients are corporations and executives who want to stand out from their competitors and manage their reputations and legacies." (My competitors might say something like, "I help companies drive sales and leverage in-house talent," or "We bring your marketing message into visual alignment to drive business.") Again, I've made it very clear what I do and how I do it. There is no mystery: If you are my target audience and I've made myself compelling to you, you'll want to learn more.

We never want to miss an opportunity to relay the benefits of our brand. While we might use an elevator pitch to talk about some of the features of what we do—in other words, the services we offer—we never want to miss an opportunity to say, "And here's the benefit my clients get," or "Here's the opportunity they have to become better because of my brand interacting with them."

Guidelines for making your elevator pitch compelling
An effective elevator pitch always comes from your heart and your head. It must be interesting and intelligent, and it should follow other guidelines, as well. It must:

- **Show excitement for your work.** If you enjoy what you do and share that excitement in how you talk about your work, you will leave that impression with others.

- **Express interest in others.** This means you ask me about myself and my work. Being other-focused makes me like you even more!

- **Sound natural.** You need to deliver your elevator pitch in your natural style and voice. Authenticity is a tremendous attractor!

- **Share examples and testimonials.** Particularly if you are in a line of work that is complicated or technical, offer a story to illustrate what you do and how you do it. I might say, "I own a national marketing and communications firm, and I start with the brand, because my clients want to stand apart from their competitors. For example, I worked with a man who was in a field where his clients saw all of the technicians at his level as the same, rather than as individuals. When he began to promote his personal brand and his sense of humor through social media, his clients saw him as more than just a 'technician'; they saw him as a personality who contributed to the team." Such stories help people relate easier to your work. Besides, we all love stories and tend to remember them after we've left.

- **Use consistent body language.** As I deliver my elevator pitch, I pay attention to my handshake, posture, eye contact and all my facial expressions. I show my confidence and the attitude of my personal brand by making and holding appropriate eye contact and engaging with a firm handshake. If I miss the eye contact and give a weak handshake, it sends a message that I lack confidence. If I want you to see me as a professional, as someone who's confident and excited about my work, but I come across as evasive or retiring, it's likely that you will remember my facial expressions and body language more than you'll remember the message that I verbally deliver. I'm looking to build consistency.

Strive to be concise, succinct and clear in your elevator pitch. If I am interested, I'll ask questions to learn more. At a minimum, I will appreciate your clarity and respect for my time.

My goal is always to leave you with a positive impression of my work and of me. In some cases, the person I encounter may not be looking for a marketing and communications firm; he may not care about branding. That's okay. At least he knows what I do and I've hopefully made a positive impression. It could be that his colleague or friend is looking for what I offer, and I want to make sure I've made a good impression so that he might be inclined to make that introduction for me.

Next steps

Let's say you've given a great elevator pitch, and now you've come to an awkward silence in the conversation. You follow up your pitch by asking your new contact, "So what do you do?" or "Tell me a little bit about yourself," and the conversation still goes nowhere. Maybe she isn't trained in delivering an elevator speech or in engaging in small talk.

If she doesn't give you anything to follow up on or inquire further about, it's safe to ask, "What do you when you aren't working?" You don't need to ask her what she does on the weekends; you don't need to ask her something that could be sensitive or personal. But everybody does something for fun. That's a perfectly safe question to ask somebody after you've made your elevator pitch.

"What brings you to today's meeting?" is another great way to find common ground. "Was it the topic? The location? The speaker?"

You might also ask, "What type of clients do you work with?" Hopefully, the person can articulate what her ideal client looks like. This question may also give her an opening to reciprocate and ask you about your client base. Either way, your goal is to seek common ground in order to build rapport.

Keep in mind that your elevator pitch is where all your brand elements come to life. The more you are consistent in your message, the more you can gain brand stickiness.

Remember, brands grow organically; they don't grow overnight. Similarly, elevator pitches take time and practice. Be patient and understand that the tenth time you give your elevator pitch is going to be a lot better than the first time.

KEY TAKEAWAYS

- An elevator pitch is a succinct description of your idea, product or service and a quick and effective explanation of how you do your work differently from others. It allows you to promote your personal brand and enables you to articulate your value proposition.

- To deliver a compelling elevator pitch, show excitement for your work. Let your passion shine through. Passion and enthusiasm are contagious!

- Strive to be concise and clear. Don't make others work hard to understand what you do and how you do it.

- Deliver your elevator pitch with authenticity. If you show sincerity, others will feel more at ease with you.

- Share examples and testimonials of your past work with clients and the benefits they received from you to paint a mental picture.

- Express interest in others. Ask them open-ended questions about their work and interests to draw them out.

- Use good eye contact and deliver your elevator pitch with a firm and appropriate handshake. Effective eye contact and handshakes make a positive impression and reinforce your stature.

12

Intentional networking

I remember my first business development job. I was given a stack of freshly printed business cards, and my boss told me, "Tonight you're going to a networking event, and your goal is to hand out every single one of these cards. I don't want you to come back to this office until all these cards are handed out." I remember thinking, "That would be easy to accomplish if I simply walked over to the garbage can and dumped them all in."

What I learned that night, and what I have learned over the past twenty-three years, is that there are two kinds of networking: There is the superficial, cover-the-world-with-your-business-card schmoozing approach, and then there is intentional networking, a way to systematically develop a network of contacts who benefit me, who have my best interest at heart and with whom I can reciprocate through a system and strategy that you will read about here.

As we have been discussing, your brand strategy must be grounded in authenticity. Remember that people do business with people. Even if a company is purchasing from another company, there are human beings on both ends of the phone call. More to the point, people do business with people they like. Building rapport, ensuring the transfer of confidential information, asking favors and reciprocating are all based on our ability to trust one another's integrity and authenticity.

The more authentic we are, the less we are like that person in the room who is simply there to make contacts and meet decision-makers. The more authentic we are, the more likely we can build genuine, reciprocal relationships.

Intentional networking is a highly effective marketing strategy for your authentic personal brand.

What networking is *not*
Let's begin by identifying what networking is not. Networking is not just something you do at a cocktail party or a business reception. It's not that guy who stands in the room shaking hands and looking over you to see if somebody more important has just walked in, then abandons your conversation. Networking is not just between business people. Networking is not just about generating leads. It is not just for professionals with large contact databases, nor is it just for people in business development roles.

Networking is about intentionally creating systematic ways you can form relationships where all the parties benefit. We all know people, but how we organize that information and how we strategically leverage our personal brand to become valuable and relevant to those contacts—that's an intentional network. While we're going to have this conversation in the context of your professional growth, there is no question that a valuable intentional network will benefit you personally as well.

An intentional network requires focus, intent and management. While your network focus is to serve your interest, which is not a bad thing, it will require giving back as much as receiving. But you will see that when we talk about an intentional network, we're not talking about the charity work that you do or the people you help in other ways. Those are philanthropic efforts that come from your heart. We are talking about a strategy that markets your personal brand.

Benefits of an intentional network

As we all know, our roles change over time. Our jobs change, our capacity and competency in our work change and our professional needs change. An intentional network keeps us on track through all those changes. An intentional network also provides a sounding board. Maybe you want to bounce ideas off one of your network contacts, or perhaps there are some deals that you're considering. A sounding board is extremely valuable in growing your professional development.

An intentional network also provides a support system, encouragement and referrals. I have landed jobs because of contacts in my network. I've gained client insight and won client engagements because of my network. An intentional network can provide valuable news and information. We all know that in today's market, this can give us a competitive advantage—the more information we have, the more power we have.

In a global environment, we have an expanded opportunity to market within international networks. What if you want to open an office in Beijing, or Mexico City, or Paris? What if you secure a new client in Tokyo? Having global connections and contacts around the world can be a valuable resource to you.

How to get started

The good news is, just like you already have a personal brand, you also already have a network. There are people whom you already know. Maybe you haven't consciously put them into any organized database, but you already have a network. Consider:

- The people you work with

- Former colleagues from past jobs with whom you've kept in contact

- Boards of directors you sit on

- Groups, clubs and associations that you currently belong to, or even that your children participate in

- Social events that you attend

- Alumni associations (Did you go to college? How about graduate school? Do you keep in touch with any of your classmates?)

Also, consider cross-functional teams. Maybe you work in marketing but you really got to know the IT team in your past job. Have you kept in touch with those people? How about social connections? Maybe your kids play on the high school baseball team. How about the other people in the stands with whom you've connected? Then, of course, there is the general public you haven't even met yet.

You already have a network. The goal is to organize it and systematically tap into the results that you are looking for.

For the purposes of this exercise, we're going to look past family and friends and neighbors for now. I encourage you to tread lightly under the guise of intentional networking when dealing with friends and family.

About you

First, look through all the areas that we just discussed—work, play, business, school, events and associations—and identify people you already know. Make a list. Maybe you have this organized in your Outlook or Entourage or even in an Excel or Access spreadsheet. Maybe it's just in your phone contact lists. The first step is to take the time and list everyone with whom you are already connected.

Second, look at your potential network: Who do you need to know? In my chapter on target audiences, we talked about identifying the audiences that need to find you relevant. Who is that target audience? If there's a prospect you don't know, write that person's name down.

Maybe in reading the morning's paper you identified someone you really need to get in front of and meet. Where does he work? What does he need, and what does he need to know about you? (That's where your brand messaging comes in!) Write that down, too.

Here are three distinct types of networking contacts to focus on. Each of these groups is valuable and compelling to you as you grow your personal brand.

Group 1: Decision-makers

We all need to meet decision-makers who can hire us, connect us to someone who might hire us or refer us directly. There is no question that meeting decision-makers is valuable.

Group 2: Information sources

Information sources possess unique information about trends, deals and industry insights. From personal experience, I can tell you that information sources have helped me secure new clients, attract better opportunities and create visibility in my personal brand. They are incredibly valuable to your ability to build credibility within a market. Some of the information sources in my network have deep experience in renewable energy, commercial real estate and financial modeling. When I have a question or need insight into a company, or I'm putting a proposal together for a firm that's involved in one of those sectors, I can pick up the phone and call these people. They're most likely not decision-makers in their organizations, and they may never hire me or refer me to somebody directly, but the information they can offer me— the insight and analysis that they can help me with—has enabled me to win business.

Group 3: Cheerleaders

Cheerleaders are contacts who will provide references, referrals, testimonials and, quite honestly, cheer me up and cheer me on. When I'm networking and I meet someone who may not be a decision maker, may not have unique industry information but could potentially be a cheerleader, I identify that person as a valuable contact. She'll be a spokeswoman for my brand. These people are my rock stars, my spokespeople and my PR firm.

I was recently at an event where I met a woman who was a former senior executive with a big accounting firm. She's a stay-at-home mom now. She doesn't have the ability to hire me and isn't likely to refer me to somebody directly. Quite honestly, her industry insight is maybe a few years outdated because she has been staying at home with her children. But she's the most positive, upbeat, encouraging person I've met in a long time, and I added her to my network—my intentional network of contacts—because of her value to me as a cheerleader.

When you think about meeting people and intentionally designing a network that will support your professional growth, move past decision-makers and look for information sources and cheerleaders, as well. Who has valuable critical insight and information that can help you personally and professionally? Who are those cheerleaders you need to add to your database because they really make you feel good, and they'll support you and speak well about your brand?

It will help to put this all down on paper. Here's an example of how you might start organizing some of your database to reflect decision-makers, information sources and cheerleaders:

Name	Company	Role	Contact Info	Met?	Notes	Next Step
Maggie Smith	ABC Company	decision maker	303.555.1212	Awards dinner	just reurned from Paris. Loves travel	call 15 July 2011
Beau Clark	XYZ, Inc.	decision maker	303.555.1213	ACG networking	has 2 boys that play baseball	f/u in 2012
Lida Citroen	LIDA360, LLC	info source	800.314.5060	Annual conference	knows about marketing yourself	sign up for her blog at LIDA360.com
Ken Scott	Acme, Co	cheerleader	303.555.1214	ABA dinner	former CPA	keep in touch via email

When you need a boost of encouragement or a client says, "I need to talk to some people who can vouch for you," you can then sort by your cheerleaders and get a good sense of who you can tap into. Or, if you have a specific proposal you're putting together or other projects and you need some industry insight, you can go quickly to your information sources. If you need to speak directly to prospects that may be able to hire you, you can tap into your decision-makers because you know they are people who have access to opportunity directly at their fingertips.

Now that you know who you would like to connect with, consider all the sources you have identified and ask yourself, "How will I get to know them?" or, "How will I get to know them better?" This is where your intentional networking strategy begins to form. This is where you start drawing concentric circles of influence: You have a network, they have a network and their network has a network of contacts. You are looking for as many opportunities as possible for those networks to intersect.

About them

To start forming your strategy, let's think about what you know about your current and potential contacts—your audience. Answer these questions:

- What do you know about them?

- Where do they hang out?

- What type of associations, groups and meetings do they belong to?

- What kind of companies are they involved in?

- What are some of their hobbies? (While you might naturally think about things like golf and some of the more social hobbies, look at all possible hobbies.)

Ask yourself, "Who do they know?" Remember those concentric circles of influence around everyone you know. Who is part of their network? Who is in their circle of influence? You need to know whom they pay attention to and respect and who has credibility with them.

Once you determine this, you want to go where your prospects are. For instance, you might join the American Institute of Architects if you're an architect or the American Institute of Certified Public Accountants if you're a CPA. Those of us in marketing might join the American Marketing Association. If you're interested in economic development and your clients are small businesses that are looking to get funding or set roots in the community, you might find an economic development group or chamber of commerce. If you are interested in women's issues, you might seek out a women's chamber of commerce.

I have joined associations focused on mergers and acquisitions or venture capital and financial services because many of my clients work in these sectors. Sure, some of the conversations might be a little bit over my head, but I'm going there because my clients, my potential clients and my contacts are there. I seek out my contacts rather than my peers when it comes to intentional networking. I ask myself: Where do I need to be seen? Where is my audience? Where do I feel most welcome?

Joining a committee can be a fantastic way to gain visibility. Let's say you want to meet speakers and influencers in the community. The program committee of an industry association could be a great opportunity for that. If you want to meet financial types, CFOs and accountants, you might join the finance committee of a trade group.

Remember that you're looking for leadership roles in these groups you are joining. You're looking for visibility. Joining an organization, attending its monthly luncheon and sitting in the back of the room will rarely benefit and promote your personal brand. This is not about making friends. If it's part of a business strategy, you don't want to hang out with the same people every time you go to the monthly luncheon. Your goal is to meet new people and to follow those intentional networking skills that we talked about. You're not just building your resume, you're looking to meet decision-makers, information sources and cheerleaders who can support and encourage you as you build your brand.

Joining an organization or committee is an obvious way to network. But there are many other ways to connect with people.

How about becoming a member of hobby- and social-interest-related groups? Maybe you are into golf, creative writing, needlepoint or dog shows. I have a very good friend who networks beautifully at dog shows. She's passionate about showing dogs, and a lot of her clients have come from her networking at those events. They have something in common. Or you can always look at something that's cause-related, such as animal rights or children's advocacy, organizations where you're going to find people who are concerned about the same issues as you are.

Sometimes networking comes from even more unusual places. For example, my son played on a high school baseball team. I noticed that some pretty high-powered professionals and executives whose children played on the same team often watched from the same bleachers as I did. I couldn't easily find a way to break the ice and network with them during games. But one time, the coach sent an email to all the parents and asked, "Would anybody be willing to work the snack shack this Saturday?" I looked at the list of emails, and there were some really valuable contacts in there. I could have replied just to the coach and said, "I'd be happy to work on Saturday," but instead, I hit "Reply to all" with my message. My email had my branded signature attached, as always.

I was, in fact, interrupting every other person on that email list with my message, and I considered that before sending the message. But in the end, three contacts wrote me back and said, "Lida, we've sat next to each other on the bleachers for months. I didn't know you did marketing and branding—we should have a conversation." I actually secured a new client out of that email. Sometimes, you have to think a little bit creatively.

As we will talk about in depth in our chapter on social networking, you also have the opportunity to connect online, and if an online strategy fits within your intentional networking strategy, there are many options to leverage. While social networking is not a replacement for in-person networking, it is a good way to share information and connect to other people.

LinkedIn, for example, removes the degrees of separation between us and multiple contacts and their circles of influence.

Facebook can connect us to childhood friends, past colleagues, fellow alumni or people who share common personal or professional interests. Both provide multiple tools to network with people who are talking about your product or service or you.

As you develop your strategy for intentional networking, look into the online networking options that align with your personal brand, your strategy and your target audience.

Where you should not network

Some places aren't appropriate for networking. I don't typically like to hang out where all my competitors are. If I'm looking for information, that's one thing, but I prefer to be where my clients are. You also do not want to network around anything that's medical or sensitive or focused on addiction—Alcoholics Anonymous meetings, treatment centers or grief programs, for example. These are not places where people want to have a conversation about business, nor do they want to be interrupted.

Sometimes you shouldn't network with family and friends. Just because somebody is your neighbor doesn't mean she wants to do business with you. Just because somebody is related to you through marriage or blood doesn't mean he wants to be asked about a sensitive project. Be careful networking with people who are very close to you, either in proximity or in familial relationships.

Measure and monitor your networking efforts

How will you know if these networking efforts are working? Because you set goals and you have a strategy. You're going to measure ROI (return on investment and return on influence), because joining an association or a professional group and getting involved has to pay off. This isn't about charitable donations. We're talking about strategic marketing and promotion of a personal brand.

You will want to periodically assess whether your efforts are producing the reputation you desire and make sure that the ROI is in your favor. When I started my company, I attended any organization, networking event, luncheon or gathering I could afford. I set a goal for myself that I would not exceed a $50 price tag. If the cost of attending a business group meeting was $30, $40, even $50, I went. My goal was to be seen and get as much information as I could. I was on a fact-finding mission to evaluate where I was going to commit my energy. If the networking events or the business forums did not include an opportunity to pass a business card or an ability to speak about what I do, it wasn't the right forum for me.

When you join, you want to get involved, so you will need to decide how much time and effort you're willing to give. In some ways it's like joining a gym: You can't just sign up and expect to lose weight. You have to commit the time and work the program to make sure you see results. What commitments are you willing to make to be involved in an association or group? You're only one person, so you're going to have to look at where your time is best spent. Make sure that you've given one hundred percent, but be sure you're getting something out of it, too. And, when you figure out which efforts are working best for you, repeat them often! One of my clients is the CEO of a successful PR agency in the Midwest. Her advice rings true for all of us: "Each day, commit fifteen minutes to promoting yourself somewhere, somehow. A small investment for a huge return!"

Personal branding networking tips
As you join groups, meet new people and expand your circle, it's very important to understand certain rules of conversation, as well as to

identify the ways you can serve your network contacts. What do they need? Remember, audiences have functional needs and emotional needs. They need things tactically delivered for them and they need emotional connections. What are they looking for? Does your audience need leads, information and insight? Do they need to feel safe, valued and respected? How are you best suited to help them? How can you make yourself valuable, credible and resourceful with these contacts?

This is how the circle starts to build. With this information, you're looking for insights that will allow you to build solid, two-way relationships with people whom you've identified as valuable contacts. As you begin to meet new people, keep in mind these tips:

- **Be open to everyone.** When you go to a networking event, make it your goal to meet three new people—that's a pretty easy goal to achieve. Be open-minded. There may be a person in the room who could provide tremendous decision-making connections for you, who could be a new information source or maybe become that cheerleader you have been seeking. You won't know unless you are open to meeting all sorts of people at that event.

- **Research people before you meet them.** If you know that someone you're hoping to meet will be at a networking event, do some homework in advance. Do a LinkedIn search; Google him to see what comes up. You're looking for opportunity to build rapport, and we build rapport based on common interests.

- **Utilize the right icebreakers and conversation starters.** Let's say you end up at that networking event face to face with somebody who has a nametag and a cocktail, and you have no idea how to proceed. A good friend of mine, Debra Fine, wrote a fantastic book called The Fine Art of Small Talk, a great resource for people challenged with finding areas of common ground that enable small talk. In her book, Debra points out that after the initial exchange of name, occupation and smiles, "Your mission is to get your conversation partners talking about themselves." She continues, "Most people enjoy the opportunity to share their stories, and if you give them the chance, they'll start talking." You never want to put somebody in a position where she feels bad about the answer she has to give you. Avoid anything that's possibly sensitive or too personal.

Among the great icebreakers she suggests that are non-threatening, you might try: "What do you do for fun?" This isn't asking what they do, or even what they do on the weekends, but what they do for fun (which is happy!).

"What brings you to today's meeting?" is another harmless icebreaker. Somebody might answer, "Well, my boss brought me," or "I thought the program sounded interesting," which gives you a great opportunity to follow up and ask, "Well, what part of the program sounded interesting to you?"

You should be sensitive to people who might be on the brink of a not-good situation because of the economy. So you can ask the question, "How is the economy affecting your business?" That might give somebody the opportunity to say, "Wow, you know what, my business is thriving!" Great—you can have a conversation about that. Or, someone might reply, "You know, the economy is really killing me and I'm on the brink of something really bad here." You can deflect and move away from that. You do not want to be associated with that painful discussion.

"What do you like most about your job?" is another option. Not everybody loves everything about his job, but you can get people talking about something with this query that might make them happy.

Other easy questions: "Are you staying in town for the holidays?" "What do you do on the weekend?" "Do you know other people here?" Always try to ask high-level, open-ended questions—not yes or no questions—to get people talking.

- **Respect boundaries:** Not everybody wants to have coffee and get to know you, or introduce you to her supervisor, or connect with you online. Not everybody wants to hang out with you at a networking event. Look for clues that perhaps this networking relationship isn't working out for her and move away gracefully. You'll gain more credibility by doing that than you will by trying to force a relationship that isn't naturally there.

I went to an event recently and sat down with a man I'd just met. He was in the financial services field, and within a few moments, I could tell I was being pre-qualified. We didn't have rapport. We didn't have any type of relationship such that he could ask me those questions about my financial situation. It would have been much better if he had noticed my unease and cut off his inquiry, instead of pushing me to the point of discomfort. Be aware of the balance between being other-focused, showing interest, and just being nosy. Walk that fine line carefully.

- **Don't share confidential information.** For example, I knew a woman several years ago who was told by a very influential contact of hers that she was soon going to be interviewed for a senior sales position within the company. Someone still held the job, but as soon as it became available, she would be interviewed. The position's soon-to-be availability was highly confidential. Unfortunately, my contact, excited that she was about to be interviewed for this high-level sales position, shared that information with someone else. That person knew the person in the job—the person about to be fired.

(If something like this happens to you, own your mistake as soon as possible. Go back to the person whose confidence you violated and let her know what happened. More than likely, it's going to come back to her, anyway. You may end up losing a relationship, but you'll maintain your credibility by taking accountability and owning your mistake.)

- **Don't assume that everyone recognizes your value immediately.** You may have a reputation that's taking some work to overcome. It's your job to intentionally create as much positive behavior in the direction of your desired brand as possible.

- **Clearly articulate your goals.** You want to make sure people know what you're looking for. There's an old joke about a lawyer and a banker who had golfed together for twenty-five years when finally the banker turns to the lawyer and asks, "Over all these years, how come you've never sent me any business?" The lawyer replied, "You've never asked." Make sure people know what you're looking for. If you're looking for a new client, if you're looking for exposure in a new market, if you're looking to be seen on stage at an industry event, be clear about how people can help you.

  When I started my business, I didn't only ask people to send me clients if they knew of any who might be interested in my work. I also asked my key contacts, who were with large corporations, to help me with my exposure. I would say, "I know you often buy tables at some of these high-profile, highly influential events, and often the seat price is over my budget. If you ever have an empty seat that you're trying to fill it, please call me. That's a way you can really help me."

- **Stay top-of-mind.** Meeting people is the first step, but even more important is keeping in touch with them once you've made the connection. Here's a great tip that I give clients that helps them follow up after meeting somebody at an event: Before you go to that event, write a blog post or a short article. At the event, when you meet somebody and you're exchanging business cards, mention that, "You know, I have a great article I just wrote on that topic we were talking about. I'm going to follow up and send that to you." Imagine his surprise and delight when he receives that as a follow-up to your conversation. Not only does it show that you're educated and informed because you offered something of value, but it indicates that you follow through on promises, which is how you build integrity.

As you develop your network, keep that contact going, and not just when you need something. When I talk to job seekers, I remind them that we hear a lot from job seekers when they are out of work, and then as soon as they find a job, we don't hear from them again. It's the same when people look for new business. Maybe the sales pipeline is dried up toward the end of the year and you're looking to network and fill that pipeline with work, but when you have enough work, you drop off the radar screen without contact until you need something again. This makes people feel used rather than valued.

Intentional networking needs to be worked. If you haven't talked to somebody in a while, if you haven't provided value to somebody in a while, you can't take it for granted that they will welcome you with open arms and provide you with leads or information or support.

- **Set up a routine system of keeping in contact.** Enter an item in your calendar that says, "The first Monday of every month, I will contact the first twenty people in my network database and tell them I was thinking about them and see what's going on, maybe drop them a note or an email, or even a phone call. Maybe the second Monday of every month, I will go to the next twenty contacts, and do the same thing." Have a system for keeping in touch with people, even if it's a monthly email that you send to everybody to let them know what you're up to.

Other ways to stay top-of-mind:

- **Become a resource.** When I meet with people, I get clues from our conversation about how I could be helpful to them. Often I visit people in their offices. Offices are typically decorated with things of interest to that person. The next time you're visiting with a client or contact, look around. Does your client display pictures of his family?

Are there framed vacation photos of him at the beach? (If so, maybe he has an affinity for a specific location.) Are there pictures of sailboats and models of sailboats around the office? Look for cues and clues about information that you might be able to share with them later.

One of my clients had a lot of pictures and photos of sailboats around his office, and I would send him articles that I came across that had to do with sailing or sailing races, and he always got a kick out of that. To him, it showed that I cared about him as a person, rather than just as a transaction.

- **As you come across articles and invitations, forward them.** People love to get information that's valuable. I use a lot of my online social networking tools to get information that's valuable for my clients—RSS feeds of a column in the newspaper, for example. Google provides tremendous tools that will push that information to you. If you focus on a specific area (maybe your business focuses on health care or education) and create a feed to get those articles sent to you, you can then be a resource to your contacts by forwarding that information to them.

- **Provide introductions.** You can't introduce everyone to everybody. But if you know a great PR executive who should know a great communications director, tell them, "I'm going to make this introduction for you," and be the facilitator. Make that introduction. It's one way to show appreciation. If somebody does something for you or has just provided valuable support or information, make sure you show your gratitude.

- **Celebrate the success of others.** Networking is about being focused on other people. Be a cheerleader for others who are in your network by congratulating them for their accomplishments and successes. (This also allows you to keep top-of-mind with them.)

- **Write notes:** The handwritten note is completely underestimated.

Most people love to get handwritten notes in the mail. I have sat with CEOs as they retrieved personalized notes from their desk drawers. Many of them recognize the time and effort someone took in sending them a personal gesture. It's beyond an email, it's beyond a typewritten note, and it is one of the most powerful tools we can use today to build relationships.

- **Be somebody people want to be around:** You're not just looking for a new client; you're looking for a relationship. Whether it's with a reporter, a prospect, a networking contact or a fellow committee member, you are building relationships and showing your authenticity. Let people get to know you—the real you—and don't pretend to be someone you're not or someone you think they expect you to be.

- **Keep networking relationships balanced.** If somebody does something for you, make sure you return the favor. It doesn't have to be lead for lead or article for article. But if somebody helps you, make sure you help him. We don't want to walk into a networking situation where the scales are tipped, either in our favor or the other's.

- **Know when to say "no."** Nobody wants to be a doormat. If somebody ask for more than she gives, it's your job to stop it.

- **Give your network time to develop.** Be patient. It's important to give your network time to grow. With intentional networking, we're not looking for one-night stands; we're looking for relationships. We're not looking for sales; we're building relationships, and that takes time. Building trust is the ultimate goal. Strive to find common ground with people, which sometimes includes small talk that's not all business.

The most important thing in intentional networking is to set a game plan, a strategy. Who do you need to know and how will you get there? It's all about sharing and collaborating. If I share an article with you and you appreciate it, send me a note. Refer somebody to me. Send me an article, or pick up the phone and tell me that you really appreciated it. It's all about give and take.

KEY TAKEAWAYS

- Intentional networking is a way to systematically develop a network of contacts that benefit you, who have your best interest at heart and with whom you can reciprocate through a system and a strategy.

- When networking, be a resource. You want people to rely on you. Look for opportunities to share information, collaborate, refer and offer something of value.

- Keep in contact. Networking is about relationships, and it requires keeping in touch more often than just when you need something.

- Respect people's boundaries. If a person seems uncomfortable with your request or unwilling to help you, recognize that you may be crossing a professional line or bumping up against her boundary for how far she is willing to go to help you.

- Reciprocate often. Whether your networking contacts are information sources, cheerleaders or decision-makers, don't forget the balance of give and take. It's not all about you.

- Follow up. If somebody has helped you, let him know how it turned out. Did you actually form an engagement with the person he referred you to? What did you learn?

- Don't forget to thank others. If somebody has really done something special for you, compose a handwritten note or pick up the phone and let her know how much it meant to you.

13

Your visual brand identity in marketing materials

In this chapter, we will dive into your visual personal brand identity: How you crisply, effectively and efficiently articulate visually what you do and what makes you stand out. Here you will learn how to position yourself with a look, feel and tone to the audience that finds you relevant.

Your personal marketing impression

Imagine you are this guy, trying to stand out in a sea of similarity. If you don't create a strategy based on your authentic passions, talents and goals, you run the risk of blending in, looking like everyone else and missing the opportunities you desire.

Your personal brand comes to life through the impression you make. Let's say I was presenting a workshop at your company. You were told that you were going to see a presentation from an expert in the field of brand development, someone who has represented leading executives, companies and organizations around the world in owning and managing their reputations. Then you witnessed a generic, uninspiring presentation and collected a boring business card from me. Would my brand impression confirm or dispel my positive reputation?

In personal branding, we can spend time and money developing our message and value proposition, defining our talents and passions and targeting our audiences. Yet it can all fall apart when it comes to presenting our brand through our marketing image. Many people have fallen into this trap in the reverse. They design snazzy websites, clever business cards and cutting-edge YouTube videos, yet when you meet them, there is nothing snazzy or inspiring about them. Their marketing impression does not match who they are authentically. It appears they just found some clever designers.

Your marketing materials should reflect your authentic brand. Often, after I've presented my program on personal branding, someone from the audience will approach me and ask, "What do you think about my business card?" or "What do you think about my logo (or colors or brochure)?" I can form quick, subjective opinions and tell her whether I like the colors, but those are just judgments. Your colors, logo, style and image should be considered in a broader context. They need to be evaluated from the standpoint of whether they support your personal brand, attract and appeal to your target audience, and reinforce your value to that audience.

I encourage you to reflect on your brand promise and your desired brand, as well as your intended audience. These are the foundational pieces of your personal brand strategy from which you can craft the look and feel of your brand. I also encourage you to think of your superhero moment. How did you show up then? When you are feeling your most confident and empowered, what look, image and colors fuel that feeling for you?

Would you find you interesting?

From business cards to websites to resumes, we all use tools to market ourselves. If you work for a large company, you won't have the opportunity to customize your marketing materials as a representative of the organization. But if you own your business, promote yourself independently or are in a job search, you have an opportunity to customize the way that you market yourself.

As you think about your visual branding, consider this question: Would you be attracted to you, based on how you market yourself?

You're trying to attract people—your target audiences—who will find you relevant, whose values and interests likely align well with yours. So, would you find you interesting, and how does that show up in your marketing?

Whenever I prepare a brand framework for a corporate, non-profit or executive client, we focus the marketing and communications strategy on tone and positioning. Your tone reflects the attitude of your marketing and how you communicate what's important to you and what you believe in. Your tone provides a filter, a set of criteria through which you'll determine, "Is this the right feel and attitude for my marketing?" All this is rooted in authenticity, but the tone really gives us a differentiator. It helps you decide if your communication is upbeat and friendly or serious and sophisticated. What is the tone you want your marketing to project?

Your positioning reflects the company that you keep and the way that you are received. In other words, what will you be known for? Who will you be seen with, interact with and strengthen relationships through? How will you position your value to your target market based on the emotional brand benefits you want them to receive from you? What is the positioning that you're looking to achieve?

You might consider your tone and positioning, for example, to be traditional, classic and timeless. You might think about brands that adopt this positioning, such as Tiffany, Crane's Stationery or Brooks Brothers. They don't show a lot of flair; there isn't a lot of going outside the box. They reflect a pretty traditional, timeless, classic, maybe even conservative type of tone and posturing. Their target audiences know they produce quality products, for which customers will spend a bit more money. Their audiences rely on a level of consistency and the emotional benefits that come with status, elegance and timeless quality.

Or perhaps you see yourself as professional, but with a slight edge. You might project a polished, clean, professional image, but with a little spin. Perhaps that spin is humor or something that's a bit unexpected. Brands like Ralph Lauren do a great job here, or Dove soap, a conservative, expected brand that uses a little bit of humor, fun and edge in its marketing. Michelle Obama is another great example of a professional brand with a bit of an untraditional edge. She's in a high profile, conservative space as first lady of the United States, yet she wears vibrant colors and trendy clothing with her arms exposed.

You might instead consider your brand to be about making a creative impact. If you're in an artistic field—a designer, a photographer, an advertising executive—you likely want to make a creative impact. You might relate to a brand like Apple computer or other companies that target creative audiences.

If you were to assign yourself to one of these three categories of tone and positioning examples, which do you see yourself aligning with best? Traditional/classic/timeless? Professional, but with an edge? Creative, with impact?

Let's say you identify with the traditional, conservative look. You might produce business cards or marketing materials that look a bit more expected. They would likely be very clean, crisp, upfront, maybe a little bit predictable, with nothing unexpected to throw your audience off. The style can be a little bit bold but still offer that professional, conservative look. These are completely acceptable, very well received marketing pieces that support the traditional, conservative look and will give comfort to your target audiences, who are likely looking for that level of reassurance from the professionals they hire.

Perhaps you consider yourself a little bit more on the professional-with-an-edge scope? When I created my LIDA360 marketing tools, I considered whether I wanted to be seen as traditional and conservative or someone looking to make a creative impact with my audiences. Those of you who are familiar with the LIDA360 brand will know that I chose the middle. My colors, tone, website, the images I use to illustrate and communicate, everything has a little bit of an edge to it. I chose bold, energetic, vibrant colors and images but retained a professional posturing and positioning for my work. All this was intentionally designed and is intentionally integrated into all my marketing materials, from my website to my business cards to my presentation templates.

If, like me, you consider yourself a little bit more in the professional-with-an-edge category, you might look at designs that incorporate some fun or whimsy. They will still appear clean and crisp, but a bit more playful. You might even consider a business card that requires a second look before you can grasp and read the information. Your marketing should be consistent with your brand image and tone to ensure it's received well by your target audiences.

Now let's say you choose to make a creative impact. You might consider marketing materials that are unconventional and have an element of surprise to them. Have you ever seen a metal business card? How about a translucent brochure? Maybe your website is an interactive flash demo of your product? If it's important to you to be seen as clever or funny or to stand out in a way that demonstrates your creative craft, you might design a brochure that wraps around pieces of bubblegum like a comic strip. The possibilities are endless; let your creativity be your guide.

The point of this exercise is that you want to make sure you stand out from your competitors, manage how you are perceived and back up the look of your marketing with your personal presence and actions.

I recently presented a speech to a group of law librarians at a large event. Afterwards, a woman dressed in hot pink leggings, a black and white polka dot T-shirt and 1950s glasses approached me. She told me, "I'm not your typical law librarian. I liked your message about individuality and self-expression and would like to get your opinion on my business cards." She then handed me a bright lime-colored business card with a clever icon and her personal logo on it. The card had very few words but a catchy tag line that grabbed my attention quickly. Without knowing her or her strategy and basing my reaction on image alone, I felt that her business cards appeared to be a clear and direct extension of the image and person standing in front of me, someone full of fun, energy and personality. It worked! It worked for her, not for the person standing next to her.

As you articulate your value, tone and positioning and begin to develop a "look" for your marketing materials, consider each piece you craft as an extension of that feeling, a reflection of the desired brand you want your target audience to experience. Each piece you create, from your business card to your website to your email signature, should reinforce the value proposition you are putting forward.

Creating shelf life for your marketing impression

While you're considering your marketing identity, also ask yourself, "Will this look have a shelf life? Will it have longevity?" If you tap into popular trends for your brand identity, you may run the risk of having to redo your branding in six months or two years. That can be confusing for your market and expensive for you. Consider something that you can live with for a while and that you'll be proud to hand out as a reflection of you. Choose an image that allows you to show confidence and creativity and all the posturing traits that you set up for yourself, but that is going to have some shelf life.

KEY TAKEAWAYS

- Your marketing materials should support your personal brand, appeal to your target audience and reinforce your value to that audience.

- Branding is about making a connection that is consistently reinforced. As you develop a visual marketing identity for your personal brand, focus on being integrated and consistent across your materials, language and look.

- Take into account the interests of your target audience. Would you find you interesting and compelling? Create marketing pieces that would get your attention.

- Strive for a tone in your marketing materials that feels authentic to you. Are you projecting an attitude of confidence, safety and approachability? Or, are you creating a tone of exclusivity and aloofness? Either way, the tone of your personal brand must come through in your marketing to be effective, and it must feel comfortable to you.

- Develop marketing materials that have a long shelf life. Unless you plan to update your materials often and have a strategy for reintroducing them to your audience, look for identity materials that reflect your passion and genuineness, not the trends that are fashionable today.

14

Your visual brand identity in personal style and image

Have you ever changed the way you naturally dress to fit in with a group? Over my career, I've dressed down to make myself blend in or worn conservative, constrictive outfits so I looked more like my peers. This usually resulted in my feeling stifled. When I learned how to express myself and highlight my passion and energy—with a bold necklace or brooch, for example—I felt more comfortable in my attire and the personality it reflected.

In this chapter, we'll focus on your personal style and image, because your style says a lot about who you are, what you value and what others can expect in a relationship with you. In your daily interactions, are you conscious of sending the right message and creating the most powerful first impression that you can?

The importance of that first impression

Have you ever heard, "You have one chance to make a good first impression"? Studies have shown that non-verbal communication accounts for eighty percent to ninety percent of the information we receive. In the first five seconds after meeting you, someone has judged you, possibly as credible, confident and professional, or as interesting, valuable and trustworthy, or as lazy, disorganized and insecure. Do you see why that first impression has so much impact on how you will be perceived?

If I perceive you as arrogant and unapproachable, I'm less likely to want to get to know you, to learn what you do and what you need. You miss an opportunity to have me help you meet your goals. Perception and judgment aren't fair. But other people's perception of us is their reality, and they will give us opportunity, assign us value and create visibility for us based on what they believe to be real.

First impressions are subconscious and judgmental. Your goal in a personal branding journey is to help other people form positive judgments about you, offer you opportunities to grow and succeed and see your genuineness and passion. If your first impression leaves an undesirable taste in their mouths, you will be quickly discounted instead.

How to best present yourself

Let's begin with a quick exercise: What impression do you think your personal style sets with other people? How do you think people view you when you walk into the room? Think of words such as confident, strong, high-energy or maybe shy, reserved, insecure" to describe what you believe your image says about you.

Write down some notes around the perception you'd like your image to create. How would you like people to see you? Would you like to be seen as friendly, approachable and confident? How about bold, expressive and creative? What impression would you like to create in the first five seconds after meeting someone?

Next, consider your target audience. How do they dress? How are they presenting themselves? Are you the only one in the room in red high heels? Does your audience typically dress conservatively and professionally? Write down some notes about how your audience presents itself.

Looking at your answers, do they align? Do you dress in a way that aligns with your desired image? And does that image mesh with what your audience expects?

I had lunch with a new client who positions herself as an innovative leader in the field of organizational development and leadership training. She targets high-technology clients who are at the cusp of tremendous growth. Her marketing materials are slick, very cutting edge. Her website has more bells and whistles than a Disneyland ride! Yet, upon meeting her, I was struck by her appearance and style. She wore a full suit (skirt and jacket) that was an outdated style and color. Her haircut was befitting someone much older and more serious. Her style was not that of someone hip and cutting edge.

In working together, we addressed a disconnection between how she marketed herself—from her website to the language on her LinkedIn profile to her marketing materials—and how she presented herself in person. Which was the real her? Bringing her image into alignment with her marketing approach and her clients' needs created the credibility she sought and removed the distraction of the disconnection.

Flair and self-expression can reveal themselves in many appropriate ways, depending on your goals and objectives. Sometimes, you want to set yourself apart from your competitors. If you have the personal presence to pull it off, you can get away with something bold.

I am acquainted with an attorney on the East Coast who is known for wearing red Converse tennis shoes. He wears them with a suit. He wears them to court. He wears them to depositions and to client meetings. This isn't a hit-and-miss thing—he's known for these red Converse tennis shoes. There's even a red Converse tennis shoe illustration on his business card, and it's a very corporate business card with this little bit of an edge to it. It's part of who he is; it's part of his style and very much reflects the way he handles himself in court and with clients. It is something that he's known for and really a part of his brand.

Ways to illuminate your personal style

Our goal is always to be recognized for our uniqueness, but not everyone would be able to wear red Converse sneakers and get away with it. Being unique doesn't mean we have to be in a clown suit when everyone else is in a business suit.

Your target audience wants you to be comfortable. In expressing your personal brand, particularly in a business setting, the goal is to show consistency with your personality, passion and interest and still be appropriate for the occasion.

Here are some tips:

- **Always dress one notch above your target audience.** If your audience wears slacks and sweaters, try a light blazer on top. If your audience wears jeans and T-shirts, make sure yours are pressed and high quality.

- **Be yourself.** Have you ever put on a blouse or jacket that a friend bought you because she loves it, but you don't? I have, and the whole time I'm wearing it I feel like I'm not being myself. On the other hand, I have put on outfits that make me feel like a rock star. I love to wear things that make me feel happy, confident and comfortable. Then I'm more easily able to be myself and engage with other people. When I'm distracted by something that someone else chose for me, something that doesn't feel right, it feels like a costume to me, and I'm sure my audience can sense that. Don't try to be somebody else. Find your own style and embrace it!

- **Choose your wardrobe for your age and your body shape.** Appropriateness means that we don't dress too young or too old and that we wear clothing that fits us well and is not distracting in a negative way.

- **Update your style when needed.** You can do this by hiring a professional stylist, reading books, getting help online or seeking counsel from someone you trust.

- **Spend money on quality pieces.** Tailor them if necessary. A small investment in tailoring could make a huge difference in how you look.

- **Consider how others will feel about your dress.** Could your wardrobe offend some people? Is the image you project creating a positive impression?

Don't miss an opportunity to relay the benefits of your brand. If you're an outgoing, approachable, confident person, make sure that shines through your image, and don't lose sight of your strategy. This is all about a plan, and it's about intentionally creating the reputation that you seek in the marketplace.

KEY TAKEAWAYS

- Style says a lot about who you are, what you value and what others can expect in a relationship with you. Think about whether you are sending the right message and creating the most powerful first impression that you can with your personal appearance.

- Strive for consistency. Create a look for yourself that is comfortable and reflects your true inner style. If you like color, embrace it. If you prefer muted tones, that's great. Whatever tone and style you choose, look for that style to reflect who you are across all of your appearance, from your grooming to your wardrobe to your complete presence.

- Be yourself in the way that you dress. How you present yourself influences your emotional state and your attitude. If you are comfortable about the way you look, your sincere, authentic personality is more likely to shine through.

15

Your visual brand image in body language

Our brand comes to life through the way that we look and act. We can learn manners and poise, and we can hire experts to teach us how to choose a wardrobe. But our body language is less conscious, though equally revealing. Our body language expresses our confidence level, mental state and emotions. It reflects whether we're scared, happy, frustrated or angry, and whether we can be trusted.

In personal branding, you want to ensure that your body language reinforces and supports your positioning and the value proposition (your brand promise) you are promoting to the world. Body language is critical. Often, we're not aware of how we are expressing ourselves through our physical presence and actions, and likewise, we can misread other people.

This chapter will take you through the importance of learning how to read, understand and monitor facial expressions, eye contact and handshakes. We're going to talk about what your body language and the body language of others reveal about a person's passion, energy level and honesty.

You may recall our first televised presidential debates in the early 1960s between Nixon and Kennedy. As the candidates approached the first debate, Kennedy was asked to put on makeup, straighten his tie and look presidential. His body language reflected his presence and confidence:

He made good eye contact with the camera, used appropriate hand gestures to emphasize key points and stood with shoulders squared to the camera. Nixon, however, had just come out of the hospital and was not feeling well. He refused makeup and any type of image consulting at the time. In turn, his shoulders were slouched, he was pale and his eye contact veered all over the place instead of directly into the camera. Over 80 million viewers tuned in to watch that presidential debate, and of those 80 million, most agreed that Kennedy won the debate, hands down. The audience that did not watch it on television but listened to it on the radio said Nixon won. That inconsistency illustrates the power of body language and appearance. Kennedy looked and acted presidential. Nixon looked sick. Listeners didn't pick up those cues in the vocal expressions, but viewers distinctly noticed the subtle but powerful differences in body language.

Effective body language starts with the face

Have you heard the expression "If looks could kill"? Maybe you've heard someone say, "He has crazy eyes," or "She has that come-hither look." Facial expressions are the easiest to read and the most revealing of our body language. It has been suggested by communications experts that you should smile when speaking, even if you don't feel like it, because that happy attitude will reflect in your voice. The way you manipulate your face reveals, and sometimes influences, what you're feeling.

Eye contact

Similarly, eye contact is a powerful tool that communicates intent, feelings and confidence. While animals are instinctively threatened by direct eye contact (if you've ever stared down an animal, you know this), it is a critical element of human communication. People have said the eyes are "the windows to the soul." Thus, it's easy to imagine the kinds of judgments that are made when someone doesn't make good eye contact or averts his eyes often during a conversation. Proper eye contact shows respect, care, trust and attentiveness. Presenters in front of an audience are often taught to sweep the room with their eyes like a lighthouse beacon because making eye contact with members of an audience is critical to building rapport and gaining trust.

It works the same way sitting across the table from someone. While a person who looks you in the eye shows that he is engaged, focused and paying attention to you, someone who doesn't make eye contact comes across as disinterested, arrogant and even superior. (If you've ever talked to someone as he is looking over your head or even looking around you for someone else, you understand this perception. In some cases, your dinner companion may have been intimidated or feel nervous about the sense of intimacy that comes with making eye contact. Regardless of the reason, it comes across as, "I'm superior to you and can't be bothered to even look at you.")

Think about how you act if a homeless person approaches you on the street. Most people don't make eye contact to avoid interaction. In a sense, you're saying, "You don't exist, and I don't have to feel guilty about not giving you money or acknowledging your situation."

The length of time that you hold eye contact is vital. Best practice says that eye contact should last two to three seconds before somebody becomes uncomfortable. If your eye contact is too short, you might be perceived as shifty or insecure. If your eye contact is too long, it can be viewed as confrontational or even sexual in nature.

As you deal with clients, prospective clients or employers, pay attention to how long you keep the eye contact and what it could be communicating about you. Make sure it's appropriate.

The handshake
In the olden days, we shook hands to show somebody we didn't have any weapons. The Romans actually greeted people by grabbing each other's forearms. I'm glad we don't do that today. Still, there are cultural differences and norms around the customs that remain. The French shake hands upon entering and leaving a room. Germans pump hands one time, and people from some African cultures snap their fingers after

the handshake to signify freedom.

The idea of a handshake is that we're creating touch, and touch can offer warmth, intimacy and personal attention or express anger and intimidation.

Whatever type of handshake you're offering, focus on making it confident and appropriate. If you've ever shaken hands with someone who gives you a flaccid, weak grip, you know it's not only disturbing but it also conveys information about that person. It sends messages of insecurity and reluctance and gives you the idea that he might be hiding something. He's offering you the weakest part of his body and communicating a lack of confidence or self-worth. None of us wants to convey that. By contrast, a bone-crushing handshake suggests domination and eagerness to compete. When someone takes your hand and squeezes so hard you think your fingers will be broken, it can be threatening, challenging and controlling. Your goal is to avoid scenarios where your confidence can be questioned and to project self-assuredness, competency and self-control with your handshake.

There's protocol for the length of time that we shake hands. Rather than using the "1 one thousand, 2 one thousand" rule, think about handshake length in terms of moments. Hold hands for a moment. Shake hands for a moment. As a rule, women tend to hold handshakes longer without feeling awkward. For men, a brief handshake is typically appropriate and comfortable. Keep in mind that it's a greeting, a welcoming.

Arms and hands

While many volumes have been written about body language related to hands, I'll review just a few ideas here. Your hands can convey many things. As speakers, for instance, we're taught to show our palms to our audience to build trust and rapport. If I put my hands in my pockets, by contrast, I might appear as if I'm protecting myself; it's a defensive measure. Similarly, if I clench or wring my hands, you could perceive me to be nervous or anxious.

If I put my hands to my face, you might think that I'm being critical and evaluating you. It can also convey insecurity, as if I'm protecting myself. Likewise, if I stroke my chin as you're talking to me, I convey that I'm contemplating or studying something. This is an accepted gesture as long as it is appropriate to the conversation. However, if I start to cover my mouth, especially while I'm talking, I send a message that I want to put the words back in, that somehow I'm not confident in what I'm saying. I would advise you to keep your hands away from your mouth—and your face—altogether, if possible.

Have you ever seen people do a "steepling" gesture, where they tilt the tips of their fingers together as if they're praying? They might believe it sends a message that they are thinking, but it actually conveys the perception that they're perhaps overly confident and maybe even smug. It could appear to others that they are disengaged and judgmental. Be careful with this gesture, unless that is what you intentionally want to communicate.

Similarly, have you ever seen someone put his hands behind his head as if he were stretching and leaning back in his chair? Often, this person will avoid eye contact at the same time. This is a very superior and off-putting posture, especially in a collaborative environment. I witnessed a client do this in a meeting recently when he felt pressured to make a decision on the spot. His body language and posture sent the message to everyone in the room that he would take his time and that decisions were to be made on his schedule. Could he have chosen a more effective way to communicate this? Sure. He didn't need to posture himself in an obvious position of authority, making the other participants in the meeting ill at ease.

We all know what it felt like when our mother wagged her finger or pointed at us as she was talking. It typically meant we had done something she didn't approve of. It was overly direct and made us feel bad. You'll want to avoid making others feel this way. If you are an animated personality and talk with your hands, as I do, make sure you show your palms up as much as possible. If you use your hands to make a point, let them complement what you say as opposed to detracting and possibly even sending the wrong message. For instance, time your hand gestures in concert with your key point, so they serve as reinforcement. Avoid pointing fingers; it could look punishing and accusatory. Instead, try using your whole hand pointed forward to emphasize key points in your message.

How about crossed arms? Have you been told that if people cross their arms, they're defensive or angry? Well, not always. In this image, you see a woman who's relaxed, who puts her arms across her chest because it's comfortable. Our most vital organs are in the core of our body and so, yes, there is a potential defensiveness or protectiveness when we cross our arms if we're feeling threatened. But it is also possible that she is just cold or is relaxed in this position, so be careful about jumping to conclusions.

What your overall body language reveals

Let's talk about what your body language as a whole says about you. In this image you see someone who is confident. He is walking with a wide stride; his hands are relaxed at his side; shoulders are back, and his head is high. This stance and posture display confidence and self-assuredness.

In this image, you see two people making direct eye contact and engaging in conversation. Their chins are tilted up, and the women appear relaxed and poised.

You want your body language to reflect confidence and composure. You want to look engaged (you're paying attention) and to carry yourself with assurance. This enables you to be perceived as open, receptive and approachable.

Approachability means having relaxed shoulders and open hands, with palms up. It means when you walk into a room, you unbutton your coat to show that you're receptive, that you're there and you're comfortable. It means that you face forward and have good eye contact. You want to show others your sincerity and authenticity. Openness means that your gestures match the context, that you're not overly anxious but you are there, present, in an authentic way.

A defensive posture, on the other hand, is one where you avoid eye contact. Maybe your fists are clenched in a protective gesture. You might cross your arms and turn your mouth down at the corners. You might be chewing or fidgeting because you're protecting yourself—you're on guard, ready to attack or defend yourself. You might have your hands in your pockets. You might also use an object, such as a lectern, portfolio or briefcase, as a deflector, a tool to hide behind. All this says that you are somehow insecure and feel defensive about the subject matter or about your position in the room.

Anger

We all know what anger looks like. Typically, an angry person clenches his fists, wrings his hands, maybe furrows his brow and even narrows his eyes. He might remain standing or suddenly stand as if ready to attack. Imagine if you're promoting a personal brand of openness, helpfulness and warmth and you display these angry gestures. You're not exactly being consistent.

112

Many people clench their jaws when they're nervous, talking through their teeth with little movement of their lips. You might think it's a way to keep in control, but it comes across as being angry and upset.

Frustration

The frustrated person paces, wrings her hands, shrugs her shoulders, exhales rapidly and often over-gestures, as if to compensate and draw attention away from the fact that she's frustrated. She might make too much eye contact, stroke her hair, finger a glass and play with a pen or other object. The frustrated person could also avoid eye contact as if she were looking over your shoulder for help or a rescue. Watch for this behavior in yourself—you could be sending the message that you are frustrated when you are not.

Boredom

Anyone who has ever had a teenager knows this look all too well. Boredom results in eyes that wander. Perhaps somebody shifts a lot in his seat, yawns, daydreams or doodles. Studies show that doodling can actually help some people stay focused, so we have to be careful not to always misread doodling as boredom. But if others are doodling and fidgeting, tapping and picking at their nails or hair, it's likely that they're disengaged. When you are in a meeting, check in with  yourself to ask if you are unconsciously doing these things. If so, you could be sending a message to the person you're dealing with that you're bored with the conversation, and for most of us, that's not the message we want to communicate.

Lying

I'm often asked how you can tell when somebody's lying. Studies of polygraph machine results reveal that when we lie, we show a certain amount of emotional arousal, as well as physical changes in the nervous system. We breathe faster, our heart rate increases and our propensity to sweat increases. Those are all physical responses that the polygraph is designed to pick up.

The polygraph is not one hundred percent accurate; neither are the best personal practices used to detect lying, though they are good attempts. Even so, watching for physical clues can help when you're evaluating someone's honesty.

One way a person who is lying might reveal that fact is with a false smile. Is she smiling with her lips, but not with her eyes? Is the smile inappropriate to the context?

The eyes offer many clues. Have you ever sat across the table from somebody with a quirky, crooked smile on his face, but his eyes are sending a very different message? Sometimes too much eye contact—a steady gaze—can be a disingenuous attempt to say, "See? I'm telling you the truth. See?" No eye contact at all can be a sign of someone who is being shifty or deceptive, as discussed earlier. Also, when we're emotionally aroused or stimulated, our pupils dilate, another clue you can use to detect lying.

Emotional pressure can also cause people to sweat, so you might ask yourself whether the person you're talking to is inappropriately sweating. She might be nervous, but she also might be dishonest.

What you're looking for is incongruity—when the body language doesn't match the message. Is the person shaking her head while saying yes? I learned this from a police officer friend years ago: Often during interrogation, a person will shake her head side to side while communicating an affirmative. The body language does not match the message. Is she fidgeting, licking her lips, or talking too fast? Are his words and body language out of sync? We're looking for deviations from the norm.

Likewise, in our own interactions, we want to make sure we're not communicating with incongruity to our target audiences. We certainly don't want to give anyone the impression we could be lying.

Gender

Let's talk briefly about how gender plays a role in body language. As I mentioned earlier, women shake hands with women differently. We're generally more comfortable with a deeper level of intimacy with other women. Therefore, women tend to hold for a longer time while shaking hands with other women. Men typically shake hands with other men based on their relationship—peers, boss/staff, colleagues, and salesman/client. The more powerful the man's position, the more aggressive the handshake might be; often, a firmer, longer and more abrupt handshake signals higher status.

Eye contact is also a type of intimacy, and becoming aware of the length of time to hold eye contact with a man and with a woman is important. Again, think moments. Think appropriateness. If you dart your eyes away too often, it seems suspicious; too long and it may appear confrontational. This is particularly true for men. When a man holds eye contact too long with a woman, it can appear to be a sexual invitation. When he holds eye contact with a man for too long, it can be confrontational, even threatening. Likewise, when a woman holds eye contact too long with a man, it can send mixed signals of her intent. By contrast, when women hold eye contact for long periods with other women, the interpretation is often that she is listening intently.

Men and women also have different tonality and cadence to their speech when talking to each other. Generally, when men talk to men, they tend to drop their voices so they sound more masculine. It's more of an animalistic-type conversation. Women tend to raise their voices when nervous or unsure, which can be perceived as apologizing.

Similarly, women need to watch out for certain subconscious body language messages, such as twirling their hair or playing with jewelry, which have sexual overtones. Men need to pay attention to habits such as jiggling keys in their pockets or fingering cups or pens. Playing with inanimate objects can send the message that you're either nervous or bored.

In reading the body language of others, be sure to consider extraneous factors that might influence how they're acting. For example:

- **Environmental factors.** What are the conditions in the room? Maybe the room is cold, and that's why the person has crossed his arms. In that case, it would be a misperception to assume he's acting defensively. Maybe the room is dark, and that's why she's leaning forward and squinting. She's not being confrontational; she's just having trouble seeing.

- **Special circumstances.** Various external factors can muddy the context and lead us to the wrong conclusions. For example, it's difficult to accurately read somebody's body language if she's nervous about giving a speech. Likewise, if you've ever seen a speaker get up to give a presentation after the last presenter went long, sometimes the second speaker appears nervous and disheveled when she's just overly conscious of the time. Or maybe she is affected by background noise. Instead of assuming that the presenter is unprepared and not credible, consider the special circumstances as you evaluate her poor body language.

- **Disabilities.** Does the person you're talking to have physical impairments that can be influencing her body language and communications? Is she suffering from a hearing loss? Does he have a nervous disorder? All of these can make a person communicate a different body language, and we need to take that into consideration.

- **Spatial relationships.** Americans typically prefer a space difference of about two feet between them and other people. Architects, engineers and urban developers follow this principle of space in designing buildings, walking paths and transportation systems. If the room is overly crowded, a person may actually be physically uncomfortable and only appear defensive. If you are talking or standing on a bus or a subway, keep in mind that a person may be uncomfortable because of a proximity issue, rather than with you or with the subject matter.

When it comes to body language, the goal is to support your personal brand with congruity. Your audience is looking for consistency. When you walk into the room, when I meet you, I want to experience the same person through your body language that I have come to expect when I read your online posts or view your website. I want to see consistency. Only then can I begin to trust that you are who you say you are.

KEY TAKEAWAYS

- Body language, your own and others', reflects emotions and sends nonverbal cues about how you truly feel.

- Pay attention to your key body language, such as your eye contact and handshakes, and what it can project. You're looking to convey confidence, not superiority, insincerity or fear.

- Gender differences play an important role in body language. Women and men have very different tolerances and tendencies when dealing with the same sex versus the opposite sex. Take note of these and adjust your actions accordingly.

- Learn to watch for ways you could accidentally be communicating through your body language that you are lying, bored, angry or frustrated. These could send powerful mixed messages to your audiences and diminish your credibility and impact.

- Body language must always be evaluated in context. Consider environmental, relational and other aspects of the situation as you draw conclusions based on body language cues.

15

Becoming your own publicist

Are you comfortable tooting your own horn?

Let's say you have your dream job today—you love what you do and with whom you work. Your clients are ideal: They pay on time and treat you wonderfully. What would happen if tomorrow it all disappeared? How would you get the word out and let people know who you are, what you're good at and why they should hire you?

This chapter will teach you how to be your own personal brand public relations agent! Who better to represent you than you?

In addition to working with companies and individuals across the U.S. and Canada, helping them launch, build and market strong brands, I have held multiple key public relations roles, either working as a PR professional or managing PR teams and agencies. I bring that expertise to my work in personal branding and corporate brand development.

In this chapter, I'll teach you how to be your own PR agent to ensure that you have visibility, are recognized for your accomplishments and achievements, and create brand differentiation so that you never compete in a lineup against others who might appear to be like you.

What is PR?

PR is how you promote yourself to others and influence a key audience. PR helps society reach decisions and function more effectively by contributing to mutual understanding of disparate groups. PR techniques can also be used to manipulate public opinion and influence large groups to see a different perspective.

In addition, PR professionals in a corporation are responsible for anticipating, analyzing and interpreting public opinions, attitudes and issues that might impact the organization as a whole, as well as for implementing the organization's efforts to influence audiences. They also counsel management regarding public policy, courses of action and communications.

In creating a PR plan for your personal brand, you will be systematically and intentionally building and maintaining your reputation among key audiences through and with the media.

Why PR is important?

A personal public relations plan is similar to a corporate PR plan. It allows you to measure success and enables you to assign dollar values to your goals. For instance, you might say, "My PR plan involves speaking at ten professional conferences over the next twelve months so that I may be known by my peers as an expert in wealth management. That would result in my landing three new clients who have a dollar amount value of X." A PR goal like this, with a timeline, gives you something to measure.

PR also helps build "third-party credibility." This is when someone notable—a key influencer or journalist—writes something about you, and audiences believe the information and assign you credibility. To build credibility for your brand, you need key influencers to speak positively about you. You need customers and potential customers, people in the community and people in your network to speak highly of you. Adding a PR strategy to your personal brand marketing rounds out the influence you have in your target markets. There are many different components to building your reputation in the marketplace and a number of strategies you can employ.

Media relations

We often think of public relations as "free advertising," but while media relations delivers your message to a target audience without the cost of an ad, there's a big difference between PR and advertising. Advertising is a paid announcement; if you want something printed in the press exactly as it's written, buy an ad. But if you want to create influence, engage others and have them understand and see your point or your mission, good media relations and a strong media strategy may be more effective. PR tells your story in the most competent and confident way, and good PR ensures you'll get fair treatment from reporters. You're positioning yourself as an expert in the marketplace.

Understanding journalists

Journalists are different from you and me. They serve a broad, diverse, vocal and highly discriminating audience. Reporters have to be able to explain your story to the general public. They are not interested in fluff. They need information that is valuable and interesting to their readers.

Try to think like a reporter instead of from your own perspective and knowledge level. Here are some important things to keep in mind as you target the media:

- **Media relations is not about securing a mutually beneficial relationship.** Reporters know you need them more than they need you. Reporters who encounter rude behavior, dishonesty, evasiveness or even a cancelled interview could blacklist you from their source files. Consider every relationship with a reporter to be a long-term investment. She may be writing for The Denver Post today, but she could be writing for Business Week tomorrow. You don't want to get on a reporter's bad side.

- **Reporters respond best to those who know the scope of their specific jobs.** Before speaking with a journalist, consider with whom you'll be speaking. Learn as much as you can about the reporter's background, topics of interest and audience.

- **Newsworthiness is key.** Just because you did it doesn't mean its news. Repetitive, irrelevant press releases will actually burn credibility more than support it. You need to have something newsworthy to talk about and make yourself relevant to the publication's audience.

  One way to evaluate the newsworthiness of your story is to answer this question: Who cares? If you can't think of anyone who would care about your story, you'll have a hard time finding a reporter who does. News means news. Reporters are interested in information that's unique, controversial, new, different and relevant to the largest segment of their audience.

- **Reporters look for sources who have track records of honesty, resourcefulness and accessibility.** Reporters try to write balanced stories, which means they may be quoting your critics and competitors as well as your supporters and happy customers. If someone criticizes you or your company and you haven't developed any credibility in the marketplace (if you don't have strong brand reputation or brand equity built with your contacts or with journalists in your community), it's likely that a reporter will be initially skeptical of your side of the story.

- **Reporters want people who have strong brands (reputations) and who may already be known by their audience.** This applies to online reputations as well as to the traditional outlets. Is your online reputation absent? Is it an afterthought? Is it skewed, or is it accurate?

- **Timing is everything.** Reporters crave groundbreaking news on their beat (the topic, area or industry they report on). They love breaking news, firsts and important new findings! They also want the facts, when they need them—immediately, not tomorrow or next week. Not providing all the pertinent details in time for deadline can kill the story or your role in the story.

- **There are no guarantees.** Not only can you not approve a story before it appears or persuade a publication to print your release verbatim, but your story may not run at all, even after the reporter has given it to his editors. Your compelling and interesting story can be bumped for many reasons: Maybe the reporter found a more appropriate source for the issue, or your story was replaced by a more important or breaking news story. (As noted above, timing is everything.)

- **Every "media hit" counts.** Many times we don't realize which media have an impact on our business; it's not always the daily newspapers or major TV news outlets. Most people strive for the lead segment on the ten o'clock news, but a hit on the Associated Press wire has a potential for placement in hundreds of papers across the country. Also, although a story in an industry trade publication may look insignificant because you might feel that only your peers will see it and not your clients, there's a snowball effect to consider. Journalists often localize or expand on stories from noncompeting media. They look for trends to illuminate for their mainstream audience by reading trade publications and local news releases. Today's Inside Supply Chain Management story could land on NBC's Nightly News next week or as an article in The Wall Street Journal.

- **Media outlets are highly competitive and want to keep their material fresh and original.** This means it's unlikely, unless you're Steve Jobs or President Barack Obama, that you will be featured in more than one competing magazine or TV show around the same time. If you attempt to pitch a story already in the works to a competitive publication, there's a good chance you'll anger all of the media involved.

- **Journalists want their stories on the front page, just like you do.** Most of them would love to get a great front page, above-the-fold piece that will earn them praise and recognition. Anything you can do to help them achieve that goal will be rewarded with fairness and respect.

Preparing for the interview

The reporter calls and you got the interview! When a reporter phones, take the time to get your notes and information in order. It's appropriate to ask the reporter, "What is the general angle of the story?" You're looking to determine why the reporter chose you to be the source, what spurred the idea. Will the interview be live or recorded? Who else is being featured in the story? Try to get as much information as possible about the story ahead of time, and always find out the reporter's deadline.

Avoid doing an interview on the spot, if possible. If the call comes in, try to schedule a time for the interview, and then take time to prepare. When asked by a reporter to comment on something, you might respond that you have some papers on your desk or you are finishing a meeting and you would like to clear them and be able to focus on the conversation. Politely ask the reporter if you can call back at a convenient time for her. Usually she will respect the fact that you're trying to get your thoughts in order, as well as your desk. In that time, search the reporter's most recent stories. Look online for any background you can find and determine which key messages you would like to get across during the interview. If you're being asked to comment on information or a trend that was published somewhere else, see if you can find that information before commenting on it.

Also, make sure you know who the reporter's readers are—this is the audience to whom you will be speaking.

Making the most of a media opportunity means following three cardinal rules:

- **Always tell the truth.** Personal branding is all about authenticity and transparency, and that couldn't be truer than when dealing with the media. Besides, it is a lot easier to remember one story than many.

- **Speak from the audience's point of view.** Anyone who is reading the publication or viewing the broadcast is considering your topic, your story and your company from a "what's in it for me?" perspective. Most people want the conclusion, or the summary, first. Then they'll listen to the supporting information. Before an interview, think to yourself, "What does the audience need to get out of this? What is the headline I want them to write about my interview? What are the three or four important factors in that point of view or position?"

- **Never share anything confidential.** There's no such thing as "off the record." Never say anything, either before taping a segment or in casual conversation with a reporter, unless you totally and completely trust the reporter.

Leveraging online media to enhance your standing with reporters

Developing an online PR strategy means that you focus on what you want to be known for. What is the reputation that you're creating? What will reporters learn about you online as they investigate whether you're a possible source?

Reporters today admit they scour social media for sources on areas they are writing about. If you are active and visible, promoting credibility and expertise in your field, chances are reporters will notice you.

I have written for several national publications and been featured in others simply because reporters and editors took note of my online activity. From discussions I started on LinkedIn to comments I made on Twitter to my profile as a contributing writer for Social Media Marketing Magazine, I have attracted the attention of notable media. The consistency, commitment and authenticity I represent online give reporters insight into who I am, what I value and where I commit my energy and passion. This makes me an attractive source for them. (We'll talk about this in much greater detail in the next chapter.)

Sponsorships

Sponsorship is another PR opportunity to promote your personal brand. Many of us who have kids are asked to sponsor baseball teams, soccer leagues or Girl Scout troops. Before you say no, consider whether the parents involved with those groups are part of your target audience. What if you're an interior designer? Or photographer? Sponsoring a group might be a great opportunity to network, not only with the sporting team or club members but also with the parents. If you're interested in the arts or museums, you might consider sponsoring an event or a specific program they offer. What if your audiences are doctors and hospitals? There are many health care and health-related events that you might want to sponsor, such as Race for the Cure, Children's Hospital fundraisers and so on.

With sponsorships, you are always looking for a two-to-one return on your investment. You want to make sure that not only are they hitting the right audience but that you are getting at least twofold out of every marketing dollar you spend. You are looking for things like signage at the event and influence with the audience. Are you able to get the database that they're emailing to? Can you make the speech from a podium if you're sponsoring an event? Even as an individual, you can look at sponsoring key events if they're going to benefit your personal brand.

Your goal in promoting your personal brand—whether through media relations, social networking or community involvement—is to promote your uniqueness and value and to make yourself memorable.

KEY TAKEAWAYS

- PR enables you to build credibility for your personal brand by getting others who are seen as reputable sources in the minds of your audience to write or speak about you.

- Effective media relations requires being prepared, authentic and credible. Talk about what you know and always be truthful.

- Online social media is as important as traditional media. Don't neglect online journalists, bloggers, social networks and forums in your PR strategy.

- PR also means getting involved. Consider sponsoring organizations or events to become visible in your industry and your community.

17

Using social media to build your desired personal brand

Whether you are just entering social media and social networking or you have been online for years, this chapter will provide unique insight into how you can use the online space to craft your intentional personal brand and broaden your reputation. Our focus will be on using social media to communicate a consistent and intentional message to your target audience.

Social media vs. social networking
Often, we use the terms interchangeably, but they are defined differently. It's important to know the differences because they will drive how you speak to the audiences that you're going to find online.

Social media refers to user-generated content, meaning it has not been vetted. The content is not produced by documented, scrutinized experts in the field but written by any person who happens to think she knows something about a certain topic and publishes something online. It might be in the form of a blog, a micro-blog or a wiki (like Wikipedia, this is a collaboration site for user-generated content not published by vetted experts). Someone might also post something in a discussion forum or comment on an online forum. Social media is also an umbrella term that covers social networking.

Social networking refers to sharing, connecting and relationship building online. It's similar to going to a networking event. You meet people online, and you share information. You decide who you want to be friends with, who you want to potentially do business with. Social networking is that part of the social media conversation where you are connecting and sharing.

Social media is an all-encompassing online conversation. You can engage in that and move your personal brand into a position of credibility and relevance by using the right tools, strategy and methodology. Like any other form of communication and marketing, it should be approached with a strategy in mind. The point of embarking on your personal brand journey is to build and manage the reputation you desire, so each piece of the plan requires strategy.

The tools offered online to communicate and network are by far some of your most powerful avenues to communicate your brand, strengths and areas of expertise. Here we'll discuss how to interact online and how to use the variety of social networking tools to find your audience and be found, assuming your target audience is also online. (You would know this after following the steps we discussed in Chapter 8.)

You can control the content
"Is there anything I can control in social networking and social media?"

I hear that question often. Most people feel that the online space is unknown and unguarded territory, and they fear a loss of privacy and control if they become visible online. Actually, you can control everything you put online. If you write a blog, contribute to a blog or post an article online, you're controlling that content. You create the information that you're putting out there.

Similar to the content you post online, you can control with whom you associate. You can choose your online friends, connections and the brands you'll attach to through online relationships. Each of those online connections and relationships reflects on your personal brand (by association).

Credibility is king online

In the online space, credibility is king. To gain visibility and recognition, you must walk the talk of the values you promote. For instance, if you say you are about collaboration, then you must engage in dialogue with others, share resources and celebrate the success of others as well as your own. The online community is extremely focused on transparency, and they'll expose an impostor in a very public way. Your goal is to create a real, genuine and engaging online persona that will attract the attention of people who care about issues similar to yours. You cannot use the online space to create an alter ego and show up as someone you're not. Stick to your personal brand plan and you won't go wrong.

Why social media works

I can tell you, without hesitation, that I have used social media tools to build my national profile. I have written for national magazines because they found me online. I have secured national and local clients because they found me online, positioned as an expert with credibility in various social media or social networking forums.

Recently, someone on Twitter posted a link to an article called "The Top 30 Personal Branding Experts." Of course, I was curious to see who was on the list. I was elated to see my name as number fifteen! I had no prior knowledge of the article's author or of this list. I looked at the other twenty-nine experts on the list and saw that I was in very esteemed company. My social networking reach and exposure increased dramatically with that experience.

How to build your personal brand online: Start with Google

In evaluating your online reputation, ego surfing or vanity surfing (going to Google or Yahoo, putting your name in quotes and seeing what turns up) will help you determine your existing credibility and visibility. You might learn, for example, that something has been posted online about you that is less than flattering. Is your name the same as a convicted felon? Maybe that's why clients aren't calling you back!

On the other hand, you might find that your online reputation is entirely absent. Nothing shows up. You wonder yourself if you even exist! This could be a result of not being intentional and focused on your online presence. The good news is that you can fix this!

First, prepare a Google profile by visiting www.Google.com/Profiles. There, you will be prompted to post information about yourself, your career and your interests. This tool is completely free and tends to rank high in Google searches. A Google profile is similar to a LinkedIn profile where you control the content.

LinkedIn

Next, become active on LinkedIn. In 2003, LinkedIn launched with a focus on business people who were looking for jobs. I hear people say they are afraid to post their profile on LinkedIn because it may give the (perhaps false) idea that they're on the hunt for a new job. But today, it's a much larger, more powerful business-networking tool that expands far beyond just job seeking. It may even shed a questionable light if you're in business and are not on LinkedIn.

LinkedIn removes the degrees of separation between people who want to connect. For example, if I know of a potential contact with a large accounting firm, I can look to my network of contacts to find out if any of them know this contact. I go into LinkedIn, type the name of my potential contact in the search field, and it returns the names of anyone in my connection network who knows this person, or even knows someone who knows my contact. Suddenly, this contact isn't so far out of reach, and an introduction doesn't have to be a cold call. Instead, I can ask someone whom I already know if he could make an introduction for me or offer insight into this prospect, which makes my efforts more successful.

LinkedIn provides you with a tool to start building your online reputation by offering space for you to write about your professional background, including your specialties, experience, education and interests. Once you've populated a profile with your photograph, summaries of your experience and education, you can start connecting with colleagues. Find people who you've worked with in the past, who you've met at networking events and who you work with currently. Send them invitations to connect and become part of your network online.

Sixty-six percent of people on LinkedIn are decision-makers who influence the purchasing at their company. Imagine if you have something that you're offering, such as market research, advertising or photography, and you're trying to reach decision-makers. It would be a missed opportunity not to utilize the tools on LinkedIn.

When I'm looking at executives or companies with whom I want to do business, I research them first on Google and second on LinkedIn. LinkedIn offers a rich professional history on each person listed. It's a great place to learn more about the person's professional background and to find areas of commonality. When you scroll through someone's LinkedIn profile, you see a wide array of information, which helps you create a positive or negative impression of that person. Recommendations, connections, comments, updates and job history give you an impression of the type of person you're viewing. Is he well connected and influential? Is he just starting out in business? Does he share and collaborate with others?

LinkedIn also provides an impressive extension to your professional networking efforts. On LinkedIn, you can join groups that bring like-minded professionals together to discuss important questions and issues within their areas of interest. These can be professional groups, alumni associations, interest groups, etc. For instance, I belong to groups like Leadership Denver, Harvard Business Review and Forbes Woman. These groups have bulletin boards where members post questions and respond to others' questions. This is an opportunity to engage in a discussion with people from around the globe who share the same business interests or professions.

Group memberships provide a big indicator of a person's interests and professional posture. If you see a list on a profile that includes groups such as Leadership Denver, Forbes Woman, Harvard Business Review and Association for Corporate Growth, for example, your impression is likely one of community involvement and professional credibility. Memberships in key groups with respected publications, industry-leading associations and trade organizations show engagement with credible voices in a particular industry. If, however, you scroll through the list and find groups like Weekend Beer Buddies, How to Make Quick Money Online and Vegas Mavens, you are left with a very different impression of the person whose profile you are viewing.

On LinkedIn and any other online social media site where you are posting information for professional positioning, you want to portray a positive picture of your involvement, contribution and commitment to the things that are important to you in business and the community. LinkedIn is not the place to share your weekend interests if they do not support the professional image you are working so hard to build intentionally. Broaden your group memberships to include a well-rounded scope of involvement.

Here are some ideas we share with clients:

- **Look for business groups that specifically talk about issues within your industry or profession.** If you are a local business, you might choose groups for entrepreneurs, marketers, sales professionals, IT experts, etc. Also, join professional associations in your field, such as the AIA for architects, AICPA for accountants and so on, and engage in the conversations active in these groups.

- **Show your commitment and connection to your local community by joining the discussion in groups in your**

area. Look for local business organizations and chambers of commerce, women's groups, local chapters of national associations and non-profits involved in areas you care about.

- **Reconnect with and promote your past to school alumni associations (almost every college, university and graduate school has a LinkedIn group online) or previous employer groups.** If you were a senior partner at the international accounting firm KPMG and are now a mortgage broker, connecting with former colleagues at KPMG could be great marketing for your new business. Plus, when I look at your profile and see "KPMG," your credibility is raised instantly because I perceive that firm to be highly credible!

LinkedIn groups are a great way to share your expertise, learn from other leaders, ask questions and bounce ideas off peers around the globe. These discussions build visibility and credibility for you as an expert and participant in a particular industry. Whether you are using LinkedIn for general professional positioning, to find a new job or to increase your client base, it is critical that people learn more about you online. LinkedIn groups allow you to intentionally create the impression of you that you desire.

LinkedIn "Answers"

Similar to Yahoo's answers, LinkedIn also has an answer board where you can check the questions that are being posed. Let's say, for example, that somebody asks, "How do I build a personal brand?" I would respond with, "I would love to help you with that," and post an answer. LinkedIn promotes me by circulating Q&A threads, and I build credibility by answering questions that I am knowledgeable about. This is a great way of connecting with others, promoting my expertise and sharing information.

LinkedIn "Recommendations"

Recommendations are another valuable asset on LinkedIn. It's important to give and get recommendations. Asking for recommendations can feel uncomfortable, but when done with tact, the recommendations will benefit you greatly. Anytime I speak at a conference or event or conclude a project with a client and someone says to me, "I'd love to write you a testimonial," I ask him to do it through LinkedIn. The reason recommendations are viewed with such credibility on LinkedIn is that you can't populate your own recommendations. The only way I can get a recommendation on LinkedIn is for the person writing the testimonial to generate and post it.

Fortunately, LinkedIn lets you review all recommendations made for you before they are published, so you can suggest edits if they are misleading, inappropriate or out of alignment with your brand focus.

LinkedIn applications
Similar to Facebook, LinkedIn offers numerous applications you can post on your profile. For instance, you can link to your blog or company's blog so that it feeds recent posts directly to your profile site; you can integrate Flikr or Slideshare to show portfolios and presentations that attest to your expertise; and you can share your reading list directly from Amazon.com to show your interests.

I'm often asked how often you should update your profile. I recommend updating LinkedIn every five to seven days, because when you update something, everyone in your network sees that update in the weekly or daily digests of contact information they receive from LinkedIn. I recommend regular updating of your profile to stay in front of your audience and remain top-of-mind.

I use LinkedIn to build and augment my professional reputation. I promote my business, the products and services that I offer and my branding expertise. I list my education and work history, but my "Summary" reads more like a bio than a resume. I've received gracious recommendations from clients, partners, etc., and they are all visible to everyone. I also use several applications on my profile and share a video that summarizes my business services. On my profile you'll also find recent posts from my blogs and a reading list from Amazon.com and resources I think are important. I promote my websites and share information that I publish in articles, guest posts, etc.

On my LinkedIn page you can see the groups and associations to which I belong. Again, I'm very active in these groups, so you see the content and answers that I contribute and the conversations around them. A lot of people are commenting on the articles that I post, so others can see that I'm growing online conversations.

Facebook

Facebook is another important way to build your online presence. At this writing, there are over 550 million Facebook users, nearly seventy percent of them outside the U.S. Most of them are thirty-five and older, and the fastest-growing Facebook population is forty-five years old. Today, the average Facebook user has over 130 friends. Imagine if you're sharing something or building a relationship with somebody in your audience and they decide to share that with their audience. That circle of influence is growing and growing!

I use Facebook to bring my brand to life and to humanize myself to online audiences. I joined Facebook at the urging of clients and colleagues who said, "We want to know who you are as a person—your lifestyle, hobbies, family." They wanted to see the human side to my brand. I took advantage of that opportunity, but at the same time, I control all the content and am very intentional about what I post. The information that you share with others on Facebook is determined by you: You can get as personal as you like, remembering, of course, that your connections will likely expand beyond immediate family and friends. Information such as your birthday (year is optional), your likes and interests, schools and career history lets your personality show through.

On Facebook, I comment on other people's pictures, posts and activity.

I'm constantly engaged in a dialogue. Before I send a post to Facebook, I ask myself, "Is this appropriate and consistent with how I want to be perceived?" If I'm not one hundred percent sure, I don't post it.

If done well, Facebook offers a great way to build a personal reputation and credibility within your network of "friends."

Business pages on Facebook
In addition to a personal profile page, Facebook offers the opportunity to have a page for a business, artist, celebrity or organization. These pages share information much like a personal profile, and you gather "likes" from followers and fans who want to connect to the page. These pages are public and can be shared by anyone. When a Facebook user "likes" a page, his network of friends sees that and can also view and elect to like the page, as well. You see how quickly and easily ideas can be shared using these pages. People who like the page can leave comments on the wall and participate in dialogues, building a collaborative network for the page.

My LIDA360 Facebook business page differs from my personal page in that it focuses exclusively on the business, rather than on me personally. Also, it is open for anyone to "like" and share. It's also open for anyone to make comments, so I monitor it to remove spam. While I don't really sell anything on this page, I do promote. I promote products that I sell in my online store, upcoming speaking engagements and other things that I offer. But I also share lots of information on personal branding that is relevant to the people who like this page. I make sure to balance the mix of informing, educating and promoting.

Facebook groups
Facebook also has groups. Groups are similar to business pages but are intended more for special interests or clubs, such as an alumni association or Neighborhood Watch program. Each group has an administrator, and members can be selected or limited, just like a club in the real world.

Blogging

Another way to take advantage of social media and gain control of your online reputation is to host a blog. If you have a Google profile, a LinkedIn presence and a Facebook page, a blog is a natural next step.

A new blog is created every second. With the number of current blogs in the hundreds of millions, I think we could all agree that the term expert is subjective. Technorati, an online publication, reports in its 2010 State of the Blogosphere that sixty-five percent of the bloggers in their study noted that they blog "for fun." The other thirty-five percent were divided among those who blog on behalf of their companies and for themselves as part of a professional effort.

I think blogs are fantastic, if done right. If you want to attract and retain readers, it's important to be clear and organized with your blog focus. In the early days of blogging, you could post an online diary of sorts and rant about anything on your mind, and readers would still likely find you. Today, with so many blogs,, yours needs a defined strategy to stand out.

The most successful (and seen) blogs are those that speak with passion and focus and have a unique personal touch. It's important to understand what your readers and potential readers will get out of the blog: Is it humor, education and information, items of interest or inspiration? Identify a topic that ignites your passion and creative energy and is something you have knowledge about.

There are many free and low-cost tools and resources available to create engaging blogs. You don't have to be a web developer to build one! WordPress, Blogger and Typepad are among the biggest platforms out there for free blog hosting. They offer templates that allow you to pick a look and theme that suit you and get right to creating content.

Just like the other social platforms we've discussed, blogging is a form of dialogue. Even though you publish the content, you want a conversation. You want people to comment on your posts and even to link to your blog in their blogs or websites.

Be sure to blog about things that are consistent with the positioning that you're building. Comment on other people's blogs. Start a conversation. Build a community around a topic.

Blog readers spend one to two minutes reading a post, so you want to make sure that your content is interesting and engaging to your audience. The ideal blog post is 250 to 750 words in length.

Twitter

Initially, I perceived Twitter to be too time-consuming, unproductive and bothersome. Also, I really didn't think I had anything relevant to say to such a broad audience. I quickly learned how to find my target niches on Twitter, build communities of interest and share information and data with peers and colleagues around the world.

Unlike a blog, which is unlimited in content, Twitter gives you only 140 characters with which to express your point in posts called "tweets." This can be tough! People who are interested in what you have to say can choose to follow you on Twitter. Your tweets are fed through all sorts of RSS (Real Simple Syndication) formats. The tweets by all the people you follow are fed into a home page that opens when you log into Twitter, or into a Twitter application that you can set up to sort and filter your incoming Tweets, or into your mobile device.

I follow quite a few people on Twitter who are on the cutting edge of branding and marketing, and when they post articles or share something, I have access to it. For many people, this makes Twitter a robust RSS feed for news, information and resources.

As the number of people you follow grows, however, Twitter can start to feel unmanageable, providing dozens of tweets per minute. A number of third-party tools can help filter, organize and aggregate all this content to keep it manageable. Hootsuite and TweetDeck are two options that allow you to create lists so that tweets on different topics appear in different lists. For example, I follow people who are interested in personal branding in one column. I track my clients in another column so that I can see what they're posting. I track people who are published authors in another column. My followers also put me into lists. I can tell by how I'm listed if my communication on Twitter is accurately portraying my own personal branding, and I check the way I'm listed often. When I see myself listed by others as "Social Media Expert," "Personal Branding," "Public Speaker" or "Marketing Pro," I know I'm on the right track with my reputation on Twitter.

You can also create keyword search lists on Twitter to see what anyone (even outside those you follow) is saying about a particular topic or keyword. And you can organize tweets to your followers. For example, you can schedule the release of your tweets ahead of time, minimizing the amount of time it takes you to post.

Twitter is a vibrant online community. If I have a question or need advice or resources, I can put it out on Twitter and my followers will respond with information.

If you visit my custom Twitter page, you can see that I have thousands of "followers." These are people who have an interest in what I have to say. I follow people, too. If you've seen my website, you can see that my Twitter page was branded to be consistent with my web page. I use the same photographs, logo and business description as on my website and other social networking sites. I'm building my brand and my online presence. I'm building consistency.

My strategy for Twitter is to connect with peers, clients, potential clients and a targeted online community while building my reputation. I allow some of my personality to come through on Twitter, as I do on all social networking sites. People want to connect with real people. Being human, authentic and expressive online gives credibility to your personal brand.

YouTube

YouTube has a large presence in our online lives. I was at a football game one night when a scuffle broke out in the stands nearby. Within about two minutes, the number of iPhones that were brought out to capture the event was staggering. When the scuffle was over, several of the spectators said, "This is going on YouTube, baby!"

YouTube is cultural. It's endemic. It's part of what we expect in our lives today. It's video sharing, information flow, awareness building, education and sales. Of course, there is another side to YouTube, but we won't discuss that here. Aside from the videos of stadium brawls, singing dogs and dancing babies, it can be a powerful tool for you to share advice, demonstrations, tips, hints and instructions with your target audience.

The beauty of YouTube is the simplicity with which you can share all of this. Let's say you're in interior design, residential real estate or web design. You can easily produce some very quick, one- or two-minute videos on best practices or suggestions to help others. You don't have to be a videographer or produce highly formatted edited content. A simple webcam or camcorder is enough to create a video of decent quality. For a small investment, you can buy a handheld video camera, something I recommend if you'll be producing videos regularly.

The ideal video length is under three minutes, because Google searches (and viewer attention spans) seem to return shorter video search results more quickly.

I have a YouTube presence to share information, educate and let audiences who may want to hire me see me in action as a speaker. I embed my videos (streamed from YouTube) directly into my website, blogs and social networking sites. My videos get reviewed and shared on others' blogs as well.

If you use the correct key words and the right tagging on your video, it can certainly increase traffic, draw attention to your and remove the abstractness of your brand.

The online space is vibrant, fast and transparent. To be active and compelling online means you start with a strategy for how you will show up, whom you want to connect with (audiences) and a commitment to being a part of a dialogue, not just a monologue.

Start engaging with your audience. You might not jump in with both feet, but participate in chat forums and start a dialogue. Have blog interaction with them. Make a commitment to relate with your audience. They must know you. They have to know where you are, and they have to see you authentically.

Here are some tips on how to manage your online efforts:

- **Get to know the three types of online audiences.** Online marketing is about building relationships, and they take time to develop. There are three categories of audiences online: "Zealots," "Influencers" and "Masses." Zealots are people who are outwardly passionate. Sometimes they're even referred to as "The Passionates." They believe in the cause, the issue, the mission, and they will fight for it until the death. These are great people to attract to the things you feel are important. You can join their movement and eventually become a leader in that movement. Gaining credibility with Zealots opens many possibilities in growing your online credibility. Zealots are obviously a group to pay attention to.

The Influencers are probably the hardest group to reach. Influencers started out as Zealots and developed a large following that hangs on every word they say. Influencers have broad reach and tremendous emotional impact on their audiences, but they're skeptical of people who might be selling through them or trying to attach to their credibility for self-serving purposes. Make sure you build relationships with the Influencers carefully.

The Masses are the everyday folks. These are people who may not be aware of an issue and aren't actively advocating anything in particular online. They can be enticed and motivated to care, and they could have a large following if properly engaged. With the Masses, your goal will be to gain visibility and motivate them into becoming champions for you and your issues.

- **Decide how much time you will spend online.** Social networking can be as time intensive as you want it to be. It is a marketing endeavor, part of your overall communication and networking strategy. The amount of time you spend in social media depends on your strategy. The more (strategic) time you invest, the more rewards you reap.

  From a personal branding standpoint, you want to spend about thirty percent of your time focused on marketing to and attracting the attention of the Zealots, the people who have passion and momentum online. Then, focus about ten percent of your time on the people who are influential and have a large following (Influencers). Again, they are hard to get in front of and are often skeptical. They have a lot of credibility at stake.

  I recommend you spend most of your time on the Masses, the everyday folks online who align with your target audience. They aren't the well-known names in the industry, but they can become engaged in the conversation in which you're interested in growing your reputation.

- **Remember to find balance.** The most important rule to remember for social media is to follow a balance between sharing, informing, asking and collaborating. Just as you would in person, you want to have a dialogue. It's okay to sell. It's okay to promote yourself. It just can't be all the time. If you were having a conversation in person and immediately started selling, the other person would likely be put off. The online space is no different. Your audience will be open to you selling if you've already built a relationship and offered useful and relevant information.

If you want to be my friend, if you want to be my connection, or if you want me to follow you, I need it to be about me sometimes. It's not all about you, and I want you to celebrate my success, too. When you congratulate me online, with a "bravo" or by sharing news of my success to your audiences, you build your relationship with me.

- **Seek the right venues for your audience.** There's certainly a plethora of sites that can be applicable for particular audiences and particular strategies. For example, if you own a T-shirt company or if you're a K-12 education company, a lot of your market may be on MySpace. Pepsi took a very aggressive marketing strategy on MySpace because its audience fit the demographic of a MySpace user and Pepsi could reach its customers on their own turf through this venue. If you have an interesting video demonstrating your expertise or your product, you might consider sites like Flickr or YouTube to house the video, since many audiences search online photo and video sharing sites for tutorials. Again, it goes back to starting a conversation with the people who need to find you and doing so where they will be looking for you.

- **Contribute to online publications as much as possible.** Make sure you reinforce your positioning by contributing often to online publications. Send press releases to online editors. See if you can write for what we call "e-zines," which are online magazines. Consider being a regular guest columnist for an online publication.

- **Research people before you meet them.** Social media offers valuable insights into the people you will encounter online and in person. A quick search through Google or LinkedIn will often reveal if you have something in common before you start the conversation with someone new.

In summary

With all the social media available, have fun and be creative. If you prefer to share information with one method over another, use that. Want to create a blog but you don't like to write? How about a video blog? You could post the videos on YouTube, on your own channel, and stream them directly into a blog. Or record your posts and stream them as podcasts if you prefer that to video. Technology continues to get more robust and user-friendly, so let your creativity run free.

If you are new to the online world, don't let that hold you back. Social media is not going away anytime soon. The web offers so many tools and resources for learning about the technical and strategic aspects of these platforms. Each of the sites we discussed has tutorials on its home page. For technical help, YouTube is a great resource with its many how-to videos, as is Ask.com and HowTo.com. For help on how to use more advanced tools and marketing strategies, Hubspot.com, Mashable.com and ProBlogger.com offer valuable insights and tips in their blogs.

If you take the time to build your initial strategy and let it guide you through your social networking journey, the details will fall into place. Have fun and be yourself. I look forward to seeing you online!

KEY TAKEAWAYS

- Be intentional and strategic in your approach to social media. What is the reputation you're trying to build? Who are you trying to build that with? Where do they hang out online? What do you most want to be known for? If you start with a strategy in mind, it will guide you through all your communication and networking and focus your time and energy toward activity that produces the desired results.

- Take control of your online reputation. Even if you simply start with creating Google and LinkedIn profiles, don't miss out on these basic (and free) tools to promote yourself.

- Strive for consistency in the look, feel and tone of what you post. If others go to your LinkedIn, Facebook or Twitter profiles and posts, make sure they see the same person.

- Remember that social media and social networking are about sharing, informing, asking and collaborating. It is a two-way conversation. Listen and learn from others. Your personal brand will shine as you stay engaged and practice humility.

- Never assume anonymity. Regardless of the control you feel you have with privacy settings, there are also many ways to get around them. Remember that this is a public space, so only share content that you want to be public.

18
Closing thoughts

Congratulations on beginning your personal brand journey! As I've written, this process is simple by all accounts, but it is not easy. There are likely parts you've struggled with, either emotionally or tactically, and other parts that came naturally. The beauty of personal branding is that it is highly personal: No two clients of mine have been the same. They have their own unique goals, values, issues, challenges and desired opportunities.

From this book, I hope you have learned that you should not wait until a crisis hits to start building that reputation. Building a credible personal brand takes effort and time; it's not something that can be thrown together in a pinch. If a job search arrives unexpectedly, wouldn't you rather have your desired reputation already underway and established?

By clearly defining who you are, how you want to be known and how you plan to live up to that brand promise every day, you put yourself in the driver's seat for your career. You attract opportunity because your decisions and actions are intentional. A clearly defined brand will help you thrive in your career in these ways:

- **Gaining credibility.** Credibility is built when you actively communicate what you stand for and then act accordingly. If you say you're open and approachable but no one can ever get in touch with you, you lose credibility. Likewise, if your door remains open but you don't communicate that value of openness, you may not get credit or recognition for being open. Building your personal brand helps you understand and then act on the values you want to project to the world, making it easier to establish credibility.

- **Staying ahead of the competition.** What is it that makes you unique and valuable in your position? It's your personal brand. Skills and knowledge can be found elsewhere, but how you do your work—how you build relationships, solve problems creatively and bring teams together to collaborate—cannot be outsourced or easily replaced. These factors secure your value to your clients or employer because you bring something to the table that no one else does.

- **Opening yourself up to personal growth.** The process of personal branding requires that you periodically measure the distance between your current brand and your desired reputation. It's a process that helps you see your strengths and weaknesses with clear vision and helpful insight. Using feedback and other tools, you'll strengthen the assets that make you unique and address the weaknesses that may hold you back.

- **Strengthening your connections.** Creating an intentional brand is not something you do in a vacuum. It requires that you create an intentional network of people with whom you share knowledge, support, ideas and even leads. When you put thought and effort into building a network that gives and takes and connects, your brand becomes stronger and more valuable—and more meaningful!

- **Improving career advancement.** Putting intention and strategy behind your actions will break you out of the day-to-day rut and help align your efforts with your goals. It will give you purpose and keep you motivated. These are the pieces that work together to advance your career and help you create the life and legacy that you want. It doesn't happen overnight, and it's never too soon to take control of your reputation and make sure you're heading down the path that you want most.

I have been fortunate to work with some of the most influential, thoughtful, committed and passionate individuals in the corporate and non-profit worlds. My clients come from all over the world. What they have in common is a strong desire to own their reputation, to create the legacy they desire and to be recognized for their contribution. Just like you.

My clients are no different from you. Some are leaders because they choose to lead. Others are influencing their industries in less visible ways. Even so, they are living authentic lives with intention and creating the laws of attraction to work in their favor. Just like you.

This book was intended to inspire and ignite your personal brand power. I hope I have created the blueprint for you to design a strategy and game plan that is right for you, personally. I look forward to hearing your feedback, reviews, questions and successes at www.LIDA360.com.

ADDENDUM:

A note to our kids about personal branding:

There they go—by car, bike, bus or airplane—off to school. Some of our kids are headed to kindergarten with their crisp Scooby-Doo backpacks resting squarely on their shoulders. Some are headed to high school, prepped with fashionable jeans, iPhones and Air Jordan tennis shoes. Others are headed to college, wide-eyed and ready to take on the world.

What they're also taking with them, these kids of ours, is a reputation. The youngsters might already have personal brands that reflect their empathy, athletic competitiveness or wondrous spirit. Our high schoolers might be "branded" as full of passion and school spirit, always there to help a friend in need. And our college students might have earned the reputation as people full of debate, curiosity and ambition.

Have they paid attention to how these reputations came about? Likely not. As they've posted their dreams on Facebook, befriended the school "rebel" or dated the "popular" girls, they've not paid much attention to the perception others are forming about them. And they should!

I have spoken to many groups of high school, undergraduate and graduate students about reputation and personal branding. Some of them still have that superhero sense of invincibility: "I don't need help with my reputation, thank you."

Others realize how important their reputations are and how important they will be in growing their personal and academic careers. Here are some tips for the kids in our lives. Please share!

- **Think about who you want to be.** Start building your intentional reputation by thinking about how you would like to be seen by others. Do you want to be recognized for your helpful nature, your giving and empathetic style? Do you want to be known for your ability to bring teams together and focus everyone on a big goal? Are you the person I'd go to if I needed someone to cheer on a project? How people close to you perceive you will determine the value they assign you. Then, your value attracts (or doesn't attract) opportunities—e.g., leadership positions at school or in team sports, admission to the college of your dreams, a great job, promotions and so on.

- **What happens on Facebook does NOT stay on Facebook.** Your teachers, college admissions officers and future employers are looking at your online profile. Facebook is "private," but only to a point. If you post something online, you give everyone you're connected to the opportunity to forward, cut-and-paste and comment on your message. Are you sure you want college admissions officers to see your thoughts about your English teacher? When my son was applying to colleges, he was sent "friend" requests from athletic directors and admissions staff from schools he was interested in. Luckily, his Facebook profile and posts were appropriate for them to review.

- **Your parents and coaches are watching, too.** When you tell your online friends that you "blew off soccer practice because I was hung over," don't be surprised that your coach is not willing to give you a starting spot on the team. If you don't want your parents and teachers to see it, don't post it online.

- **Be aware of guilt by association.** In the world of reputation management, who you hang out with directly affects others' perceptions of you and whether they will find you valuable and give you opportunities. To people who may not know you well, seeing you form friendships and relationships with people, groups, organizations and clubs that have questionable or controversial values makes others think you do, too. If you hang out with people who smoke pot, I assume you do, too. If you hang out with groups that serve the community and help others, I assume you do, too. It's as simple as that.

- **Put your best foot forward.** How you show up is as important as whether you show up. If you show up to class dressed sloppily and too casually, your teacher might think you are disengaged and "checked out." The same goes for a work environment: If you don't dress up to the part, you can send the wrong impression.

- **Instead of focusing on how others present themselves, find your own sense of style.** If you prefer things more traditional, strive for a classic wardrobe. If you like the energy and fun of trendy fashion, then go there—just keep it within reason. Showing your midriff in class is akin to wearing a tank top at the office: It is inappropriate and distracting. I see the midriff, not your value.

- **Listen to feedback.** Gossip is often hurtful and untrue. Sometimes, however, gossip can become valuable feedback about your personal brand. If you hear through the grapevine that you're thought of as a "party girl" or a "slacker," you could be doing something to create this perception. Could it be the way you're dressing? The way you're talking online? The people you're hanging out with?

- **A negative reputation can prevent others from giving you opportunities you want.** If you are thought of as a "slacker" and you really want to compete for college scholarships, will your teachers be inclined to write recommendations for you? Why should they?

- **Use the feedback you receive and gossip you hear to keep yourself**

focused on how you want to be known. Become intentional about what you do and how you show up to move in the right direction. Avoid situations, people and groups that drag you in the opposite direction.

Your personal brand—your reputation—is one of the most powerful and empowering parts of your identity. You can control how others think and feel about you by what you say and do. If you say you are committed to serving others, make sure you do. If you want your teachers to see you as engaged and committed, be sure to show up on time and be ready to go.

I received this nice note from a former Army officer I had the pleasure of working with on her personal branding. In our work together, she related much of what she was learning from me to how she was raising her thirteen-year-old daughter. Here is what she sent, six months after we finished her personal branding work:

"I'm still working on my brand, more so with my daughter. I keep trying to let her know there is no need to be part of the crowd. She's too beautiful to become invisible. "Mom, what are you talking about?" she says. I say to her, "If you act, dress and try to look like everyone, then you will never stand out." Lida, I thought about you when I was giving her this life lesson! "

None of this is easy—but it is simple. Getting a start on personal branding as a young person, when many patterns of behavior have yet to be set, gives your reputation the ultimate potential.

CASE STUDIES:
Personal branding in action

The following are sixteen case studies from clients I have worked with in recent years. (Their names have been changed to respect their privacy.) Through our discussions, all these clients found their unique and remarkable selves and learned how to project and market their personal brands in ways that brought them desired opportunities. Their stories are deep and robust, but they certainly do not represent the entirety of our work together; I have taken key elements from their backgrounds to illustrate a point to you in each one. My hope is that you will find some of yourself in their stories.

Bob: A CEO with vision and passion... and a heck of a nice guy
Bob is, by all accounts, one of the nicest people you'll ever meet. He is warm, approachable, hospitable and personable. Everyone knew Bob as a "nice guy."

Bob is also CEO of a highly successful technology company that serves children in the education system. Bob is deeply passionate about innovation and is schooled and versed in education technology. He has committed his life to improving the education system in the U.S. and has created numerous technologies and systems currently in place. But at the time his public relations team hired me to help, he wasn't credited with many of them.

The problem was that being known as a "nice guy" didn't reflect what he had accomplished and what made him credible as a formidable "thought leader" in his field.

In redirecting Bob's reputation beyond "nice guy," he and I began with a deep inventory of his brand assets, the things he has done that make him credible as a thought leader in the education industry. After a personal brand audit and brand feedback assessment, we identified specific and compelling opportunities to broaden his exposure, fine-tune his audience focus and begin to target his personal brand in a more intentional way.

The game plan we developed included creating a new vernacular for him to use to articulate his thoughts and position. For instance, I directed him to speak of his work with terminology that could articulate his vision for "disruptive" and innovative technology (e.g., using words like innovative systems instead of processes), elevate his stature and clue in the audience that he is introducing new concepts, not simply advancing the status quo. While his audience of educators needed to warm up to this new language, they took note of the bold and elevated way he now discussed his vision for change. They noted his increased confidence and the more impressive way he presented himself. (Image consulting and counseling on body language also helped.)

His audience began to see his passion, appearance, tone and style as that of a thought leader and not just a colleague they enjoyed being with. A key moment came for Bob at a large education conference he attended along with peers, vendors, industry leaders and his staff. During a general session presentation, a speaker whom Bob greatly respects pointed to him from the stage and said to the audience of several hundred people, "There, my friends, is a true visionary in our field!" Bob knew then that his personal brand was finally being recognized.

Bob is still a very nice person—the kind of man you'd be fortunate to know and even more fortunate to work with—but he is also becoming known for his expertise, passion and commitment to education technology. He is a sought-after speaker at international events where thought leaders gather. Most important to Bob, he is able to broaden his voice in advocating for education reform and innovation, which is his true calling.

Gail: Finding her voice through her personal brand

Gail originally approached me to help her decide if she should abandon her current business model and create something completely new. She owned a successful design firm but was not sure she retained the vision and passion for her work that she had when she built the business twelve years earlier. She wanted to do something different and thought her personal brand might enlighten her to that path.

When we inventoried her passions and vision for her life and how her values supported her credibility in her work, we actually found more synergy than she'd anticipated. We learned this through questions such as:

- What makes you truly happy?
- What are you proudest of?
- Where have you felt the greatest success?
- What is the most flattering feedback you've received?

Gail's responses showed that she was truly passionate about providing solutions, holding her clients' hands through stressful processes and being outdoors in nature. These were the things that mattered most to her.

Next, we issued a feedback survey to her key colleagues and clients. We asked them brand-related questions, including:

- What do you think Gail's personal brand is?
- Would you refer Gail to someone else?
- If so, how would you introduce her?

Her feedback survey revealed many gems, including the revelation that her target audiences appreciate her patient style and ability to reassure and validate their needs and to make a complicated and stressful process smooth.

Armed with this information, Gail took hold of her business model and modified aspects to leverage her strengths, passion and talents. We developed an integrated brand marketing strategy for Gail and her business, which included blogging, authorship, public speaking and new client sectors. She intentionally leveraged her passionate, caring and focused style on serving her existing clients in a more robust, targeted way and extended the reach of her services to companies and groups involved in sustainability and natural resources, to feed her need for connecting with the environment.

While in the past Gail would have focused on delivering quality product on time and on budget, assuming her clients appreciated that service delivery model, today she is seen as someone in her industry who brings value-added insight and analysis to her engagements. She still meets her clients' budgets and goals, but she is in high demand for her thought leadership. Her clients now see her passion and claim it is contagious!

Cathy: Something isn't sitting well

When Cathy called me from Boston, she had a problem. She was about to pull the trigger on a new website for her consulting business, and something just didn't feel right. She couldn't put her finger on it, but something about the new website didn't sit well with her.

Together, we decided that a personal branding project was in order. Cathy's business leveraged her reputation and her personal credibility. It was a direct extension of her personality, reputation and network of contacts. Therefore, it needed to match up closely with her personal brand. Knowing this, I chose not to look at the website design until after we had done our work together.

Through this work, I learned that Cathy was passionate about action. She talked fast, ran ideas together quickly and was attracted to clients who were very Type A—energetic and results-driven. Cathy was upbeat, happy and creative. A successful sales executive for many years, she had an extensive network of high-performing clients and prospects.

After assessing the results from her brand feedback and dissecting the functional and emotional needs of her audiences, we learned that her target audiences truly appreciated the fact that she moved fast, produced results and delivered a high degree of transparency to her process.

Then I looked at the website mockup. No wonder Cathy's stomach hurt! Her website designer had chosen subdued colors, passive imagery and header copy that read, "Are you tired and burned out? We can help." How uninspiring and demotivating!

In her brand framework documents, I had provided Cathy with new language, marketing direction and tone suggestions. We shared this framework with her web designer, and although Cathy couldn't figure out why the website didn't feel right to her, within a couple of weeks the designer came back with a home run! The new site reflected her energy and attracted the attention of her dynamic target audience; the copy was bold and direct, just like Cathy. She told me months later that her website became a true reflection of who she wanted clients to get to know. The mistake she'd made, as she described it, was focusing on "decorating" before building the "foundation."

Robert: Needed more exclusivity across the board

Robert is a successful and highly sought-after venture capitalist. His expertise lies in helping second-stage private and non-profit entities position for the next round of growth, whether that is funding, IPO or organizational restructuring. You can often find Robert participating in a panel discussion or presenting at various corporate growth, mergers and acquisitions or executive business events and conferences. He is well known in his industry and very difficult to get in front of.

Robert enjoys the limelight and attention he receives from his public speaking and authorship of white papers on forward-thinking funding mechanisms. Often, after a presentation, there is a long line of audience members seeking a few minutes with "the expert."

So why was Robert chatting it up and offering advice on Twitter? "I found Twitter one day and thought it was a hoot! How fun to meet professionals and entrepreneurs across the world. So what if they ask me for advice online?"

Robert sought me out because he was receiving indications that his personal brand was lacking focus. He feared he had spread himself too thin, had not stayed true to his beliefs and was not attracting the types of engagements he enjoyed.

In our work together, we clearly identified that Robert's "sweet spot" came from the exclusivity and stature he'd earned as a noted expert in his field. His social media efforts (willfully sharing advice and insight to the masses on Twitter) were inconsistent with this positioning. To maintain his exclusive stance and his reputation as a highly discreet confidant to successful entrepreneurs who paid dearly for his talents, guidance and insight, we needed to put some social media guidelines in place. Offering this type of information in such a retail-facing environment could damage his exclusive positioning.

Our strategy for Robert including limiting his online social networking to a strong LinkedIn presence, his personal Facebook page and a proprietary blog (set up with passwords) directed toward his target audience. This strategy enabled Robert to be easily found on Google searches and in social media rankings, but it retained his value proposition with a specific niche market.

Clark: Twenty years a CEO, now needs to detach his brand from the company

For more than two decades, Clark had been nationally synonymous with a well-known company in his industry. He had authored fourteen books, testified as an industry representative in front of the U.S. Congress and spoken at more than 200 international events on behalf of the industry and his organization. His well-known name and body of work were regarded as leading edge and a change agent.

Now, Clark faced retirement from his role. It was time. The organization needed new leadership, and Clark needed a new passion in his life. His successes were well recognized, and the future was truly his to own. He would be working as an industry advocate and visiting scholar at some of the top educational institutions in the world. All his new work would be under his name, not the organization's. Our challenge was to detach Clark from his company and reinvent his personal reputation in the eighteen months before he left the helm.

In doing so, we created unique and compelling messaging and a targeted set of goals. He had earned recognition, albeit under the company name, but would now need to leverage his familiarity to create new opportunities.

After carefully considering his authentic personal brand assets, the key audiences he enjoyed and had stickiness with and market opportunities to create change, we began a process of public relations, thought leadership development and networking to build his individual personal brand. We positioned Clark on the platform at key industry events; we devised a new series of books he would write highlighting his expertise and unique voice; and we positioned Clark in key leadership roles within non-profit entities around the world that furthered his passion and his mission.

The result is that today Clark is well known and regarded for his individual contribution to the industry and has the respect of peers and fellow thought leaders.

Richard: Positioning his reputation in a new industry

Richard had spent the previous thirty years as a high-profile finance executive, raising funds as a venture capitalist and investing in a specific technology industry niche. Numerous international media outlets profiled his unprecedented success and business acumen and labeled him a "pioneer" and "innovator." Notable conglomerates had acquired each of his portfolio companies, and his net worth reflected his success. He seemed to have a sort of venture capitalist Midas touch.

Five years ago, Richard and his family traveled to the Third World, and he was personally touched by the devastation and depletion of natural resources there. Richard returned to the U.S. and began exploring and understanding the sustainability field and the opportunities for both investment and impact to sustainability.

When I met Richard, his question was: How do I turn my professional focus to align with my growing personal focus? If he moved too quickly in the direction of his new passion, he could lose the faith of investors and colleagues whose money he was responsible for managing.

In our personal branding work, we discussed the passion/differentiation/ brand asset piece of Richard's personal branding first. Clarifying and detailing his passion for this new venture was critical. In the VC world, opportunists are everywhere: They sniff out the next best idea and jump on it! For most of his competitors, greed is king and opportunity can represent greed. To Richard, this was a personal calling, not an opportunistic play. It was very important that we not move too swiftly or inauthentically, or colleagues, investors and media could see him as disingenuous.

Instead, we crafted an eighteen-month strategy for Richard. He needed to build a carefully constructed bridge between his experience and expertise and this new passion for sustainability. We used various tools to bring his voice forward in a way that would not disrupt his current business: We started a blog for him, in which he shared the story of the Third World trip and his awakening to the importance of responsibility to natural resources. We began a program of intentionally introducing new language to his repertoire. He began to casually mention his passion for sustainability to key colleagues and peers. He started attending key events in impact investing on his own time and telling friends, colleagues and blog readers about his learning. He also began personally contributing to and supporting companies that were leading the way in a manner that aligned with his values. Subtly and slowly, we brought his passion forward, allowing his voice to become louder. Soon, he began linking to his personal blog on sustainability and impact investing issues on his business email.

Eighteen months later, Richard was actively serving on the boards of two high-profile companies in impact investing, and his blog had a tremendous following. He was asked to comment on an article in Harvard Business Review on the topic of value in creating communities that focus on sustainable practices. Richard found himself living in a space that felt more authentic and intentional in his life and legacy.

Sandy: Finding her voice in business

When I first met Sandy, she was reluctant to talk about "all this branding stuff" because what she needed instead, she said, was a corporate identity package for her new business. She had left her post as corporate counsel for one of the largest consumer goods manufacturers in the U.S. and was beginning a consulting business around corporate communications. She wanted marketing pieces, not messaging.

But when I shared the value of creating the messaging first, Sandy understood that her marketing pieces and collateral would have greater meaning and impact if we focused on her vision and passion before looking at fonts and colors.

Going through the personal branding process—identifying her values, competitive advantage and target audiences—clarified several things for Sandy. First, she began to articulate why she didn't like working in some companies and with certain types of clients and why other companies and clients made her enjoy her work and want to give more. She realized, for example, that she truly enjoyed working in male-dominated industries where her voice would be unique, rather than typical. She enjoyed being "special" and different. She also realized she wanted to work with clients who were focused on action, not just talk. Clients she had worked with who enjoyed long process and slow movement frustrated her. Her sweet spot was with companies that needed solutions quickly and were prone to act swiftly.

In this way, she was able to pinpoint the specific programs she felt most passionate about offering. These were the ones that attracted the most attention and gave her the most reward, personally and financially.

When it came time to design and develop a complete corporate identity package, from logo to website, for Sandy's business, we based everything on her passions, values, vision and target audience. As we hit each sample and proof, we'd ask, "Does this look and feel like the Sandy you want others to see?" Giving Sandy the filter and the power to make intentional decisions freed her to successfully launch her business and never look back.

Christine: Self-editing was the key

Christine was amazing by all accounts. In her late 20s, married with no children, she was the national vice president of sales for a large technology conglomerate. She traveled extensively, often to participate in meetings with her much older peers. The question that seemed to come up in every business encounter Christine had was "How could you be so young?" Christine feared that her age was undermining her credibility with her peers, clients and prospects.

After I personally got past the fact that I was meeting a beautiful, young, talented woman whom I envied for her passion, enthusiasm and abilities, I began helping Christine figure out how much of the age issue was external and how much was internally driven.

In our work together, we included a feedback assessment. The colleagues, clients and supervisors who responded to Christine's request for feedback gave her glowing reviews. They noted her abilities, talents, sales acumen and business savvy. They also noted that she seemed young for her position and that she often seemed to apologize for her youth.

In speaking to me on numerous occasions, Christine obviously assumed I was wondering how she could have achieved such success so early, and she often apologized for her age. In crafting our strategy, my first recommendation was for her to stop mentioning it in business conversation. The more she apologized for her age, the more it confirmed suspicions others might have had, or worse: It introduced the notion when it never existed in the first place.

Changing this behavior was not hard for Christine. She focused on editing out comments that referred to her age, and she learned to embrace the fact that she was proud and confident, not apologetic, about her success. We worked on her body language and professional image to ensure that she was current with her wardrobe and confident in her gestures and movements. When someone did mention how young she appeared for her position, she learned to answer, "Thank you!" and move on.

Within months, the age comments lessened. Christine actually learned to embrace her youthfulness, knowing that as she aged it would become less novel.

Jackie: Was her online persona dead?

Shortly after a presentation to executives at a Fortune 100 company, Jackie, who had taken my advice and Goggled herself, contacted me. She had typed her name into Google, with parentheses around her first and last name together, and the results shocked her! She learned that a woman with the same name—same spelling and middle initial—was the victim in a high-profile murder case on the East Coast. This woman's name and image had been featured in numerous news publications in print, television and online. The woman even looked a little like Jackie!

Jackie was rightfully alarmed. She worked in a sales/business development role and believed me when I told the group during the presentation that potential clients will Google you to learn more about you. She contacted me for help with her online persona and reputation.

Jackie and I worked through the personal branding process, with a focus on how she wanted to be positioned online. Her first comment: "Alive!"

Good point.

In directing her online persona, we established that there were several points and places online that Jackie had neglected: She had not updated her LinkedIn profile in months, her Facebook status went without updates for weeks at a time and she rarely posted on the blog or Flickr accounts she'd set up.

Since our first need was to ensure that people searching for Jackie found my client—the live one, not the dead woman in New York—we looked at any and all opportunities to show her vibrancy and liveliness wherever her potential and current clients might search for her.

We used several techniques to do this, including:

- Jackie began using her maiden name spelled out as her middle name. This name was different from the murder victim's name.

- Jackie reactivated her dismal Facebook account, made the viewing settings "public" and reconnected with friends and work colleagues. Then, she set a schedule to post at least once a week, if not more.

- She posted comments on industry blogs, the company blog and on listserves in her field.

- She updated her LinkedIn profile every four days with news, awareness-building pieces and updates about her career.

- She became active in industry groups on LinkedIn, often posting discussions and responding to discussion posts.

- She began a blog about her field and her climb up the corporate ladder in a traditionally male industry.

Each of these actions was designed to amplify her online persona, highlight the fact that she was active and alive, and build an online reputation that was consistent with her values and goals.

The result was that news footage of the East Coast murder was not the first result Google populated when users searched for Jackie. She reclaimed her online identity and lives happily ever after.

Aimee: Struggling with Asian cultural boundaries in marketing to the U.S.

Aimee is an Asian businesswoman who is an accomplished account executive in the tourism industry. She had been personally responsible for major campaigns and initiatives to attract tourist interest and dollars to areas such as the Middle East and Singapore. Based in Abu Dhabi, Aimee now wanted to pursue similar job opportunities in the U.S. tourism market and realized she had cultural norms to overcome in learning how to market herself effectively in America.

We worked together on her personal branding over Skype (much as I would have loved to travel to the Middle East!) and quickly identified several of the issues with which she struggled. Aimee's issues were common to other clients, many who are Asian executives, with whom I've worked. They all had strong cultural connections to navigate when amplifying their personal brand power.

First, Aimee needed to embrace a "self-focusing" approach to positioning herself. She was raised with the understanding that the team/company/community/family is more important than the individual. While this is valid, the premise of personal branding begins with a deep understanding and appreciation for the unique qualities of the individual, not the team, and what that individual has to offer to the team, company, community and family.

I helped Aimee see that putting her needs and values out front enabled her to understand how she could add value to the organization. This is a good thing! This makes the company and the community better. She learned that focusing first on herself meant she was able to contribute at a higher level.

Next, we looked at how we could package and promote Aimee's unique qualities and skills in a way that differentiated her from her competitors. She was now competing in an American marketplace, where terminology, reputation and skills are very important. We needed to package her international experience in a way that created a unique value proposition and made her stand apart. This kind of "self-promotion" was foreign to Aimee and made her uncomfortable at times.

We spent a lot of time understanding the functional and emotional needs of her American audiences. Through research, interviews, discussion and surveys, we learned what we needed to do to meld her audiences' needs and her abilities and experience in a marketing approach.

Our targeted and focused strategy meant she would position herself more effectively and proactively, projecting confidence and humility at the same time. Contrary to her previous approach of sending resumes and waiting, we were now going on the offensive and marketing Aimee as a unique asset who was highly sought after.

Aimee is a very authentic, approachable person, and when she saw how her genuineness could still shine through while she aggressively marketed herself, she felt more empowered and in control of her job search process. At the time of this writing, Aimee is considering whether the move to the U.S. is, in fact, her passion. Either way, she is designing a legacy and reputation for herself that is authentic and compelling, in whatever country she decides to call home.

Candice: Separating her personal brand from her company's

When I first met Candice, a successful East Coast businesswoman, I was impressed with her confidence, high energy and award-winning career. She had taken a small ad agency and turned it into the leading graphics and promotions firm in the education field, with an emphasis on social media and technology. Now, she was nearing retirement and needed a strategy to leverage all her success to ensure the longevity and identity of her firm.

At the time, the viability of her firm depended on her being actively involved in every step. She realized how closely tied together her personal brand was with the company's and wanted to make sure that the two could live independent of each other should she decide to retire and/or sell the company.

In working together, we learned several things: 1. Her feedback showed that the company's brand was closely tied to Candice's personal brand and credibility, as she'd suspected; 2. Her company did possess brand attributes separate from her personal brand that were marketable to new audiences; and 3. Candice needed to clearly articulate how she made certain business decisions, such as staff and client selection, to ensure the successful succession of those who took over.

Interestingly, the most valuable part of her personal branding came when we clarified Candice's personal values, as opposed to those of her business. We identified the five key values Candice held most dear, those that must be present for any venture, relationship, project or idea to be successful and personally rewarding. Using this "filter," we began applying a "what would Candice do?" filter to every business and personal decision: "Would that decision be authentic and consistent with my values or would it look and feel like I was straying from what I truly believe in?" she asked herself often.

In articulating her personal values on paper, she embarked on an interesting approach to succession planning: Candice crafted her written obituary, as well as the message that would be sent to her staff immediately upon her passing. In these written pieces, Candice talked about her passion for the work, her vision for the company and her desire for the staff to keep things moving forward in her absence. She laid out steps they should take, in detailed order, and the ways they could keep the values of the organization thriving under new leadership.

In her personal branding work, Candice had become clear, thoughtful and intentional about her daily interactions with clients and prospects. I checked in with Candice a few months after we finished our work. Here is what she reported to me:

"Since completing my personal branding work, I have fired three clients—they drained our energy and were not a match for our values! I've written my succession plan, hired three new team members who are amazing... and received seventeen inquiries for new work in the past three weeks! The 'law of attraction' really works!"

Greg: Ensure I'm doing right by my clients

Greg had a good thing going. As a senior partner in one of the nation's largest employee benefits firms, his clients were loyal and his appointment calendar full. New business came his way steadily. When Greg and I first met, he shared with me that his main goal was to ensure that what he was doing—and how he had been working for the past twenty-five years—was the right way going forward. He wasn't looking to fix anything that wasn't broken.

Our personal branding work brought forward the reasons behind Greg's success: His clients greatly appreciated his candor and honesty. They found him to be highly focused on their needs and not on selling.

Several clients shared that Greg had built solid relationships across their companies, not just with decision-makers, showing how much he cared about each client as a company and not just as a paycheck. They shared numerous stories of how Greg offered pro-active recommendations, even when they were at a financial disincentive to him, and how he was always accessible to them and ready to answer any question. His clients viewed Greg as a true "advisor" and stakeholder in their companies' future, not as a sales agent.

In creating his strategy, we didn't change any of this, but simply turned up the volume, so to speak, making it easier for him to leverage his assets. For example, we developed a structured database to help Greg track, monitor and update client information (his previous methods included "sticky notes" and writing notes on napkins), which allowed him to remember birthdays, special occasions and other important dates more efficiently. We structured his in-person networking to be more focused and intentional, rather than casual and by happenstance, so that he could leave less to chance than before. We also created a tracking system, so that he could follow up and monitor the effects of his networking. We then set him up with an account for an electronic communications tool so he could regularly schedule e-newsletters and announcements to his client database. This tool also allowed him to stay top-of-mind with prospects, promoting his "high touch" and approachable value proposition.

These tactics and the overarching strategy were manageable and fun for Greg, and they took hold immediately. Within weeks, his clients began forwarding his communications to prospects he should meet, and he received very positive feedback from prospects that appreciated his attention to relationships, not just a sale. For Greg, personal branding revealed the many things he was doing right, so he could confidently and effectively continue to market himself in ways that felt authentic and produced great results.

Jane: A student who found her path

When I first met Jane, she was a second-year law student simultaneously earning her MBA at a major university. A bright and beautiful young woman, she had earned honors as an undergraduate and served in the Peace Corps before law and business school. She was the kind of hopeful, talented and ambitious young woman who mothers wanted their adult sons to date!

With her whole future in front of her, it became clear in our first few meetings that she had a lot of anxiety around how she would make decisions that "felt right" to her. She had to find her voice and personal brand. As we talked, every other sentence from her was, "My father says I should ... " or "I've been told I'm good at ... " or "It makes sense that I should ... " Rarely did Jane relate anything that sounded like her own beliefs, values or desires.

It became clear to Jane that she had not articulated her path or vision for herself. When we began to clarify her values and her passions and talk about how they could shape the choices she made and how she would leave her mark on the world, she began to cry. "No one told me I could think this way!" she exclaimed. "I only knew what I was good at and how to make a living at that." She suddenly felt she had more options.

When we began to detail her values and personal brand on paper, she saw the simplicity of her personal brand as a filter. She could easily point to other areas in her life that were now out of alignment (e.g., "deadbeat boyfriend") and felt excited about the changes she would make. She told me that this filter, her personal brand, empowered her more than her esteemed education: "I see options that feel right to me! I don't want to work in the attorney general's office. I want to work in the international aid effort overseas. Now I know why!"

It was uplifting and encouraging to see someone as bright and talented as Jane find her direction so early in life. I keep in touch with Jane and watch her progress. Seeing her follow her path clearly and with intention is one of the highlights of my work.

JT: Career military officer disabled in Iraq transitions to corporate America

I met JT along with several of his colleagues during a week-long workshop I ran for disabled U.S. veterans in the Wall Street Warfighters Foundation program, which helps veterans train for and secure jobs in large Wall Street firms.

JT had been tall, handsome and outgoing—a true Texas gentleman. He had been in military intelligence in the Army before being injured and losing both legs in combat. His return to civilian life had been a difficult transition, despite his gregarious and seemingly happy personality.

JT didn't know how to take what he had learned in the service and translate it into a successful job interview. He found it difficult to explain his past career choices, his military experience (much of which was highly confidential) and his goals for a future career. He struggled with sharing too many details of his involvement in the Army or not enough to keep someone interested.

We needed to translate the skills and abilities JT had learned as a career military officer into relatable and differentiating skills and talents that would attract financial services hiring managers.

We took inventory of his work in the service and the way he personally approached that work. His collaboration skills were one particular quality that kept coming up. JT excelled at team-building and getting buy-in from members of his squadron at all levels. Combining his leadership skills, dedication to task and exceptional education, we articulated his personal brand as a leader, collaborator and someone you would enjoy working with. We were able to show potential employers what a passionate and accomplished financial professional looked like, one who had valuable collaboration and team-building skills.

JT was hired by a prominent Wall Street firm and is building his career in equity trading. Today, he markets himself with intention as he looks for his next job. He recently passed the Series 7 exam (scoring ninety-three percent!) and is well on his way to a successful career in financial services.

Charlotte: Doubled her business in six months

After a successful career in corporate business, Charlotte decided to market herself as an organizational and executive coach and consultant. She was well networked in the corporate community, and her connections in business were the envy of those who knew her. So what was the problem?

As Charlotte explained it, she lacked focus around the goals, clients, work and vision for her consulting practice. She did not have a process or filter for hiring staff, pursuing new clients or communicating the value of the company with current clients. On top of all that, she was feeling more and more dissatisfied with the quality of the clients she was attracting.

In our work together, it became very clear that Charlotte had spread herself and her value proposition too thin. While she had a contact database many people envied, she had taken on projects that did not leverage her strengths ("but the fee was attractive!"), had networked at too many unrelated industry events and had not marketed her value proposition to the right target audience.

She needed clarity and knew the work started with her personal brand and reputation. She wanted to ensure that she was staying true to her authentic self while taking advantage of all her assets and focusing her efforts to produce the highest returns.

First, we worked on clarifying her value proposition: What was she passionate about? What was she truly "best" at? What did she want to be known for? How would her positioning give her personal and professional happiness?

Then we focused on the types of clients she enjoyed working with the most: What did they have in common? What industry/location/business were they in? What did they appreciate the most about her work? Where did they meet and gather?

Focusing her strategy on the principle of "like attracts like," I sent her on a new mission in her business: She would strive to work less but be more focused and command a higher rate of personal and financial return. Charlotte began interviewing prospects who called on her. Instead of being grateful for every new lead, she took responsibility to ensure that they were a fit for the company first. Charlotte recognized the clients who gave her group the most positive feedback and the most satisfaction and took on those clients, while turning away the others. Taking control gave Charlotte an important new filter. This made sense!

Within six months of finishing our work together, Charlotte reported that her business had doubled. A mutual colleague asked her if she had created a new logo or website that was the impetus. "No," she responded, "I just got very clear about what I wanted and who I wanted to work with. It all starts with me." Thus her intentional personal brand was launched.

Mara: Unleashing her physical assets as part of her brand

The founder and CEO of a Canadian-based non-profit, Mara was used to living on airplanes and speaking in front of large audiences around the world. It was not uncommon for her to address a school district in Australia, then hop on a plane and speak at a convention of educators in Los Angeles later the same week. She built her reputation as an international expert who helped educators around the world teach children with autism.

Mara possessed many strong and compelling personal assets. The one she was most hesitant about, however, was her appearance. At six feet tall, Mara also had deep green eyes and flaming red hair. There was no hiding it when she entered the room. She commanded attention simply by her presence. Unsure of the appropriateness of this attention, Mara typically wore her hair pulled back in a low bun and little or no makeup to understate her appearance.

In her personal branding work, we surveyed her colleagues, clients, peers and staff to assess how her reputation stood. We looked for feedback about what was working and what needed fixing, to move Mara closer to her desired brand. Surprisingly, her feedback revealed something interesting: Her audiences noted a feature of Mara's that they found to be enlightening and memorable. Her most notable feature, they proclaimed, was her striking, unique appearance! They loved her red hair and height. Mara considered her strong presence to be a liability, when in fact her audiences found her to stand out wonderfully in a sea of "sameness." Her audiences loved the fact that she stood apart and was so bold.

With the help of a professional wardrobe consultant and stylist in New York, our personal branding unleashed Mara's comfort with her physical assets. Her appearance now complements her passion and energy for her topic and has given her renewed confidence. Mara still needs to be respectful and careful not to overwhelm audiences, but allowing her natural physical attributes to become part of her signature look made her even more memorable and effective to audiences around the world!

ABOUT THE AUTHOR

Lida Citroën is an internationally regarded branding expert based in Denver who has made a career of helping people and companies create new or enhanced identities. With more than 20 years of experience, Lida is a brand architect who excels at finding and emphasizing the values that operate at the core of each company and every individual.

In 2008, she launched LIDA360 to create corporate marketing and personal branding strategies that have authenticity and durability. These 360-degree brands are built to continuously revolve around client needs and intuitively evolve to meet business objectives, positioning people and companies to outpace the competition. Lida's personal branding clients range from recently downsized executives who want to change the focus of their lives to public speakers looking to differentiate their value from competitors to returning war veterans entering the civilian the workforce.

Prior to launching LIDA360, Lida served as chief marketing officer and brand leader for national associations, international consumer product companies and numerous professional services firms around the U.S.

As an accomplished speaker on building personal brands, her programs, consistently generate rave reviews and have built her following in-person and online.

Lida's work has attracted the attention of FOX31 News, ColoradoBiz

Magazine, KUSA- Channel 9, The Denver Business Journal, Forbes.com and national consumer and trade publications, who have highlighted her expertise in social media marketing and brand development.

Lida and her husband, Scott, live in Greenwood Village, Colorado. While their boys are spreading their wings in college, Lida and Scott keep occupied with their two "other kids" -- Golden Retrievers Hailey and Heidi.